Strange, Amazing, and Funny Events That Happened during the Revolutionary War

Jack Darrell Crowder

This book is for the thousands of students I taught over the years.
Teaching was the best job I ever had.

Copyright © 2019
Jack Darrell Crowder
All Rights Reserved.

Printed for Clearfield by
Genealogical Publishing Company
Baltimore, Maryland
2019

ISBN 9780806358833

Table of Contents

Introduction………………………………………………………......4

Chapter 1 - Gathering Clouds of War 1765-1774………………..…..5

Chapter 2 - Shots Fired and No Turning Back 1775…………...…...13

Chapter 3 - Dark Days of War in the Northern Colonies 1776-1777....31

Chapter 4 - The Winds of War Begin to Change 1778……...…..………55

Chapter 5 - The War Shifts to the South 1779-1780……………........63

Chapter 6 - Victory and in Time Peace 1781-1783…………...…..…..85

Chapter 7 - Strange Events……………………....……………..….…..109

Chapter 8 - Notable Facts of the Revolutionary War……....…..…..125

Bibliography………………………………………………...…..……131

Index……………………………………………………………...…...141

Introduction

When I was in school my favorite subject was history class, which could sometimes could be very boring. The teachers seemed to have little passion for the subject, and with each chapter we were required to memorize the same things. These included names of the major people, important dates, important battles, causes of the event we were studying and the results. It was history, the stories about dead people and dead events.

Yet I enjoyed history, because sometimes I could find in the book some weird obscure event that made the story interesting. I began reading other history books, always looking for the unusual or some fact that seemed too strange to be true. When I decided to become a teacher, I wanted to make the unusual a part of every lesson.

I taught World History in high school for a few years. As I organized each lesson I would research stories about the events or people that would make them come alive. I believed that these stories, lost to mainstream history books, would add awe and in some cases humor to the lesson. I believe this made the people, who were long dead, appear to have really lived. When I was successful, students might say they couldn't believe that it really happened that way.

The purpose of this book is to teach the reader some history from a different angle and perspective. If I'm lucky maybe the reader will want to read more about the person or event. So sit back and get ready to read some crazy and outlandish stories about our Revolutionary War that you didn't learn in school or find in most books. At the end of each story I cite some sources that contain specific information about the event. These sources may be found in the full Bibliography at the end of the book.

"If one could make alive again for other people some cobwebbed skein of old dead intrigues and breathe breath and character into dead names and stiff portraits. That is history to me!"

----- George Macaulay Trevelyan

Chapter 1

"All the friends of Liberty may have an opportunity of paying their last respects to the remains of this little hero and first martyr to the noble cause...." A report on the death of Christopher Seider, February 1770.

Gathering Clouds of War – 1765-1774

In the early 1760's most colonists thought of themselves as British. English was the official language, the legal system stemmed from British common law, many towns were named after hamlets in England, and the two countries shared many of the same holidays and customs. Yet, differences between the two peoples began to grow.

The colonists had their own legislatures that were somewhat independent of the King. The colonists could pass their own laws, raise troops, and pass local laws. This began to give some of the people the belief that these political powers were their rights. Soon the British Parliament felt a need to curtail the power of the colonial legislatures. After all, the British believed that the colonies were created to serve the needs of the crown, and their colonial subjects should bow to their demands.

When the French and Indian War (1754-1763) took place, King George III went into debt when he provided supplies for his army to defend the British colonies in America. To pay for this enormous cost the King began to impose taxes on the colonies without their consent. This led to resistance from some of the colonies. British goods were boycotted, which led to tension between the colonists and British soldiers.

On February 22, 1770 an angry mob was protesting at the house of Ebenezer Richardson, a customs service employee. When the mob began throwing stones at the Richardson's home, Ebenezer responded by firing a gun into the crowd. Eleven year old Christopher Seider was hit and later died. Over 2,000 people attended the boy's funeral, where more hatred toward the British was stirred up by the rhetoric of Samuel Adams.

Public outrage continued to boil over leading to the Boston Massacre. On March 5, 1770 British soldiers shot and killed several colonists in a protesting mob that had threatened them. The soldiers were later tried and were either acquitted or given reduced sentences, which further angered the colonists.

Paul Revere's propaganda version of the Boston Massacre in called *The Bloody Massacre*. The Customs House (on the right) has been renamed "Butcher's Hall" and a small gun can be seen firing from a window. This gun is in reference to the death of Christopher Seider.

In December 1773 the colonial resistance movement struck again in Boston. Members of a radical group, the Sons of Liberty, destroyed the entire shipment of tea sent by the East India Company. They dumped 342 casks of tea into Boston Harbor, while many Bostonians looked on.

Parliament responded to this act of defiance in 1774 by passing the Coercive Acts, better known as the Intolerable Acts. These drastic measures ended self-government in Massachusetts, and they closed Boston harbor to trade. The colonies answered the British threat by establishing the First Continental Congress. After much discussion the Congress sent a "Declaration of Rights and Grievances" to King George. They hoped the King would give in to their demands and avoid further hostilities. Most people in the colonies were opposed to seeking independence. However, a small group of radicals began to encourage freedom from England and the establishment of a new nation.

The First of Many Deaths

Christopher Seider may have been a ten year old bystander on that cold day in February 1770. However, he became the first American causality of the forthcoming American Revolution. His death set into motion other events that would lead to war between England and her colonies.

On February 22, 1770 a large group of school boys and apprentices were picketing the shop of Theophilus Lilly, who was a merchant who had chosen not to boycott British goods. Local patriot leaders had organized the protest, and the names and addresses of merchants who would not support the boycott had been published in the Boston newspapers. Some merchants had been chased out of their shops and beaten, but the protest at Lilly's shop had been peaceful.

The group of boys began harassing Lilly by throwing rocks, snowballs, and ice at his shop and his customers. They even hanged Lilly in effigy in front of his store. Things began to get out of hand with the appearance of Loyalist Ebenezer Richardson.

Richardson was at one time a confidential informer for the Loyalist government and later for Customs officials. In the mid 1760's he became an official Customs' employee, enforcing the laws against smuggling, and helping to collect hated taxes. He was a known and unpopular man in Boston.

Ebenezer Richardson lived nearby and rushed to Lilly's store to help the merchant disperse the crowd. Instead, the sight of Richardson aroused the crowd even more. More stones and other objects were thrown at Richardson, and one object caused a gash on his head. They chased him back to his home and began throwing objects at his house. Windows were broken, and Richardson's wife was hit in the head by an egg. Richardson was furious, and while standing in a second story window he aimed a musket filled with buckshot at the crowd below. He threatened to fire if the crowd did not disperse.

He fired his musket and later claimed that he intended the shot to be a warning, but he hit two boys. Sammy Gore who was nineteen years old was struck in both thighs and a hand. Christopher Seider was hit by eleven pieces of lead shot described as the size of peas, and they struck the young boy in the breast and abdomen. Doctors attended to the boy, however, he died about nine that night.

The following account of the event was published in the Boston Gazette three days later:

"On Thursday last in the forenoon, a barbarous murder extended with many aggravating circumstances, was committed on the body of a young lad of about eleven years of age, Son to Mr. Snider of this town. A number of boys had been diverting themselves with the exhibition of a piece of pageantry near the house of Theopolis Lillie, who perhaps at this juncture of affairs may be with the most propriety be described by the name of an IMPORTER. This exhibition naturally occasioned numbers to assemble, and in a very little time there was a great concourse of persons, especially the younger sort. One Ebenezer Richardson, who has been many years employed as an under-officer of the customs, long known by the Name of an INFORMER, and consequently a person of a most abandoned character, it seems, took umbrage at the supposed indignity offered to the importer and soon became a party to the affair. He first attempted to demolish the pageantry, and failing in the attempt, he retired to his house, which was but a few rods from the exhibition. Several persons passing by house, Richardson, who seemed determined to take this occasion to

make a Disturbance, without the least provocation, gave them the most opprobrious language, charging them with perjury, etc. which raised a dispute between them. This, it is supposed, occasioned the boys to gather nearer Richardson's house, and he, thinking he had now a good colouring to perpetuate the villainy, threatened to fire upon them, and swore by god that he would make the place too hot for some of them before night, and that he would make lane through them if they did not go away. Soon after, a number of brickbats or stones were thrown among the people, from Richardson's house, but the witnesses, who were sworn before the magistrates, declared that it did not appear to them that till them any sort of stack was made by the people on the house. This, however, brought on a skirmish, and Richardson discharged his piece, loaded with swan shot, at the multitude, by which the unhappy young person above-mentioned was mortally wounded, having since died of his wounds. A youth, son to captain John Gore, was also wounded in one of his hands and in both his thighs, by which his life was endangered, but he is likely to soon recover of his wounds. We were assured that not less than 11 shot were found in the body of the unfortunate boy, who was inhumanly murdered by the infamous informer on Thursday last. It is hoped the unexpected and melancholy death of young Snider will be a means for the future of preventing any, but more especially the soldiery, from being too free in the use of their instruments of death."

After the shooting Richardson was hurried off to jail, otherwise the man would have probably been beaten to death. Samuel Adams, always looking for some way to stir up more hatred against the British, saw a golden opportunity with this tragic event. He paid for and helped organize the boy's funeral four days later, which turned out to be the largest ever held at that time in America. The people assembled at the Liberty Tree, where Samuel Adams had attached a board with the following message,

"Thou shalt take no satisfaction for the life of a MURDERER—he shall surely be put to death and

Though hand join in hand, the wicked shall not pass unpunish'd."

Cropped version of "The Colonists Under Liberty Tree," illustration from Cassell's Illustrated History of England, Volume 5, page 109 (1865).

The funeral procession stretched more than half a mile with over 2,000 people in attendance. There were more than four hundred carefully groomed very angelic schoolboys marching two by two, cloaked in white, and leading the coffin. Six boys carried the coffin followed by the boy's family and friends. The funeral and the speech by Samuel Adams fueled public outrage that peaked eleven days later with the Boston Massacre.

Ebenezer Richardson was convicted of murder in the spring, but the judges delayed his sentencing because they hoped he would receive a pardon from London. A pardon was received a few years later, and Richardson began a new job with the Customs Service. The pardon was granted saying that Richardson acted in self-defense.

Phillis Wheatley, a young slave girl about sixteen at the time of Christopher's death, later wrote a poem about the event entitled, *On the Death of Mr. Snider Murder'd by Richardson*. She became the first African-American woman to publish a book and the first to make a living from her writing.

Sources: 1. *Discovering the American Past: A Look at the Evidence, Vol I: to 1877* by William Bruce Wheeler, Lorri Glover. 2. *Founders: The People Who Brought You a Nation* by Ray Raphael. 3. *Bill O'Reilly's Legends and Lies: The Patriots* by David Fisher. 4. *In Pursuit of Liberty: Coming of Age in the American Revolution* by Emmy E. Werner.

A Lame Excuse

Around 1762 young Nathanael Greene began experiencing health problems. Most notably asthma, which kept him awake most nights. His right knee began to swell often and stiffen without cause or reason. He later wrote that, *"was not enough to prevent me from running, jumping, or wrestling with the strongest of active companions; but enough to be seen a limp in my gait."*

Nathanael was allowed to join the American army as a private, but the lame Quaker was not considered "officer material." His courage and leadership was later noted and he began to rise in the ranks. Major General Nathanael Greene, second only to General Washington in military ability, was instrumental in defeating the British in the south and bringing the Revolution to a close. He became known as Washington's most gifted and dependable officer.

Sources: 1. *Forgotten Patriot: The Life and Times of Major-General Nathanael Greene* by Lee Patrick Anderson 2. D.A.R. Lineage Book, Vol. 59, page 288.

National Archives

Next Time I Will Remove My Coat

When George Washington was a young man he was about 6 feet 2 inches tall, 175 pounds, and had large hands and feet (size 13 shoes). He was a strong and powerful man, as demonstrated in this story told by the artist Charles W. Peale. Peale was a friend of Washington and had painted nearly sixty paintings of him. One of the first paintings was in 1772, when this story takes place.

"One afternoon several young gentlemen, visitors at Mount Vernon, and myself were engaged in pitching the bar, one of the athletic sports common in those days."

[Pitching the bar was a game of strength, a log-throwing, or pole-throwing, competition similar to the tossing game played by Highland Scots.]

"Suddenly Colonel Washington appeared among us. He requested to be shown the pegs that marked the bounds of our efforts; then, smiling, and without putting off his coat, held out his hand for the missile. No sooner did the heavy iron bar feel the grasp of his mighty hand that it lost the power of gravitation, and whizzed through the air, striking the ground far, very far, beyond our outmost limits. We were indeed amazed, as we stood around, all stripped to the buff, with shirt sleeves rolled up, and having thought ourselves very clever fellows, while the Colonel, on retiring, pleasantly observed, *'When you beat my pitch, young gentlemen, I'll try again.'"*

Source: 1. Recollections and Private Memoirs of Washington by his Adopted Son George Washington Parke Custis, page 519.

Free Tea, Just Jump In

Sarah Fulton and her husband often visited her brother Nathaniel Bradlee in Boston, Mass. On December 16, 1773 a group of patriots met at the Bradlee house when Sarah and John were there. Sarah and her sister-in-law had made costumes for the men, so that they would be dressed as Indians and then they stained the men's faces red.

National Archives

The men went to Boston Harbor, and they dumped 342 casks of British tea into the water. They returned home and the two women washed the stain from their faces. Sarah Fulton is sometimes known as the Mother of the Boston Tea Party. After the Battle of Bunker Hill Sarah was placed in charge of the wounded soldiers. Later George Washington called upon her to take a message through enemy lines when she did. Sarah is this author's 7th great grand aunt.

Sources: 1. *Women Patriots of the American Revolution a Biographical Dictionary* by Charles E. Claghorn. 2. D.A.R. Magazine: American Monthly Magazine, Vol. 17, 1900.

Vengeance is Mine Sayeth the Hills

The reason that Henry and his brother Nicholas Hill joined the army at the young age of eight and ten occurred in 1774. Their father Henry, a fearless patriot, made a remark in the presence of British military officers, which was construed by them as disrespectful to their King. For that remark Henry was overpowered and unmercifully whipped in the presence of his wife and his two sons.

The indignities and insults heaped upon their father angered the two boys, and they were determined to avenge his treatment the first chance they got. In the winter of 1776-1777 they joined Captain Aaron Austin's Company of the 2nd Regiment as drummer boys, and were in active service until the end of the war.

They served in the 1st New York Regiment which was organized in New York City in 1775. The boys participated at the Battles of Saratoga, Monmouth, and they witnessed the ceremony of the surrender of Cornwallis at Yorktown. They were engaged in active Indian service under Major Peter Ganzvoort at Fort Stanwix, and under Colonel Van Schaick, and General John Sullivan in the famous Sullivan Expedition. In 1779 Nicholas officially enlisted in the regiment and was discharged in 1783.

"I enlisted at Albany in the state of New York in the year 1779 in the company of Captain Douglas Blucker Colonel Van Schaicks Regiment called the 1st Regiment as a drummer for during the war. I continued in said company and regiment until the close of the war."

The first important service Nicholas performed soon after he enlisted, was when Colonel Ganzevoort sent him with a message to headquarters at Albany about a possible Indian attack on Fort Stanwix in the winter of 1777. Nicholas was sent with a young man named Snook, who met with an accident and had to drop out about half-way through the journey. Nicholas discovered that he was being pursued by Indians, so he ran all night through the snow and delivered his message the next day. He later described his thoughts as he approached Albany that morning, *"the smoke from the forts and houses stood up through the still morning air like a forest of ghostly white tree tops."*

Nicholas was at Valley Forge during the winter of 1777-78. The next year he spent the winter at Morristown. This was known as the "Hard Winter" because of the harsh conditions. On January 3, 1780 a heavy snowstorm hit the camp. When tents blew off, soldiers were *"buried like sheep under the snow…almost smothered in the storm."* The weather made it impossible to get supplies to the men, because many had no coats, shirts, or shoes and they were on the verge of starvation. *"For a Fortnight past the Troops both Officers and Men, have been almost perishing for want,"* George Washington wrote in a letter to civilian officials dated 8 January.

Nicholas told stores about the suffering of the troops during that cold winter. He said on one occasion the army was near starvation, and rations of a gill of whiskey for each man was distributed. A big Irishman named Valentine kindly offered to share with him his own ration, and he gave Nicholas about a teaspoon of the whiskey. Because Nicholas was in an exhausted condition the small amount of spirits overpowered him, and he laid down apparently lifeless. The Irishman took him on his back and carried him for miles until they reached a place that could provide proper treatment for Nicholas.

Washington at Valley Forge

The hardships of Nicholas and his brother Henry caught the eye of General Baron Von Steuben. The General was aware that the boys' parents had died soon after they entered the army and offered to adopt the two boys. The boys declined the offer. After the war both boys received a pension for their service.

Sources: 1. U.S. Pension Roll of 1835. 2. Tombstone 3. Sons of the American Revolution Application. 4. Pension Papers W11284. 5. *Heroes of the American Revolution and Their Descendants: Battle of Long Island* by Henry Whittemore, pages entitled Hill and Allied Families. 6. D.A.R. Lineage Book, Vol. 142. The University Magazine, Vol. VIII, #1 New York January 1893. 6. Pension Papers W23279.

Chapter 2

"What a glorious morning this is!" Comment by Samuel Adams to John Hancock at the Battle of Lexington, April 19, 1775.

Shots Fired and No Turning Back -1775

The British government refused to yield to the demands of the newly formed Continental Congress. Parliament declared that Massachusetts was in rebellion, and the British navy blockaded the ports of the colony. Other punative measures were employed that affected all of the colonies.

The American people began to quarrel among themselves over what actions they should take. Many of the colonists in New England began encouraging armed revolt against England. Some of the people in the middle colonies looked upon the problems with England as a New England problem and were opposed to a revolution. Most of the recent emigrants to the colonies were supportive of the King of England. Some merchants saw ruin if they did not break from British rule, while others saw ruin if they did break.

In 1775 the American colonies divided into three camps. One group were the Radicals or Patriots, who sought independence from England. A second group were the Loyalists or Tories, who remained loyal to the crown. The third group were neutral and would at times gravitate to one side or the other, depending on how it would benefit them at the moment.

As problems with Great Britain began to rise, Massachusetts saw the need to have special units who were ready to turn out at a minute's notice when there was an emergency. The Provincial Congress passed a resolution on October 26, 1774 for the formation of minutemen. It stated that the militias in Massachusetts enlist companies to *"hold themselves in readiness on the shortest notice from the said committee of safety, to march to the place of rendezvous..."*

The minutemen were volunteers, who trained more often and were usually paid an average of one shilling each time they trained. They usually served until the emergency was over, which at most times was a term of several days. Many of the minutemen that served in the Battle of Lexington and Concord served for around five days, and because the threat continued, most enlisted in the militia for eight months. Their officers, like in the militia, were selected by vote, and most of the time the leading citizens were named officers. Men that served in the French and Indians War were also given positions of command. Strangely enough Lexington did not have a minutemen company, but rather they had a militia.

Who were these minutemen? Most were farmers and shop keepers with practically no military experience. The majority of the minutemen were under the age of thirty-five, and some were even teenagers.

Tension began to increase between the colonists and the British and it reached the boiling point in April of 1775. Men like Samuel Adams were doing everything they could to start a revolt. Militias were being organized, and arms and ammunition were being hidden away in anticipation of fighting between the Patriots and British. Tempers began to flare between the patriots and the Tories. On April 14, 1775 the British Commander-in-Chief and military governor of Massachusetts, General Gage, received orders to disarm the local militias. The King also ordered

Gage to capture the offensive Samuel Adams and John Handcock and ship them in chains to England to be tried for high treason.

In a surprise move he sent a force of British regulars to Concord to capture the supplies, and at the same time capture Adams and Hancock who were in the area. This would end talk of a rebellion and prove to the traitors that British rule was not to be taken lightly.

Resistance was met at Concord and Lexington, and men on both sides were killed. More British troops were killed as they marched back to Boston from Lexington. After the British had returned to Boston they soon found the city surrounded by 15,000 militiamen.

The American army consisted of these militiamen many who would be returning home in a few weeks. They had only six working cannons, a shortage of gunpowder, one tent for every twenty men, and a food supply that was running out.

In June of 1775 the British landed troops at Charlestown, Massachusetts, and the Battle of Bunker Hill began. The result was a very costly British victory. A few days after the battle, Congress commissioned George Washington as Commander-in-Chief of the American Army. The first military objective of the newly formed army was to gain control of the British Providence of Quebec. The adventure ended in American failure in December of that same year.

Even with hostilities going on in the colonies, many Americans hoped that a large war could be avoided. But on August 23, 1775 King George declared all the colonies to be in a state of rebellion. The British army had been purposefully kept small since 1688, as protection of abuses of power by the King. Parliament now begins to negotiate treaties with various German states for additional troops to be sent to the Americas. The Revolution that few wanted had now begun.

Early American Trash Talking That Nearly Started the Revolution

British Lieutenant Colonel William Leslie led an attack on Salem, Massachusetts on February 26, 1775, nearly two months before the battles of Concord and Lexington. The purpose of the attack was to seize provisions, gunpowder, and cannons that the Patriots had stored there. As the British marched on Salem that cold Sunday morning the alarm quickly went out through the town. The 240 British regulars, with the drum and fife corps playing Yankee Doodle, marched toward the bridge over the North River at Salem.

Colonel Mason of the American militia had the northern leaf of the drawbridge raised to stop the British. On the south side of the bridge stood the American minutemen armed with muskets, pitchforks, and clubs defiantly facing the British regulars.

Colonel Leslie called out to the Americans, *"I am determined to pass over this bridge before I return to Boston, if I remain here until next autumn."*

Captain Felt of the American militia replied, *"Nobody would care for that."*

The British Colonel yelled back, *"By God, I will not be defeated."* Captain Felt answered, *"You must acknowledge that you have been already baffled."*

Colonel Leslie then said that he was on the King's highway and would not be prevented from passing freely over it. An old man in the crowd yelled back to the Colonel, *"It is not the King's highway, it was built by the owners of the lots on the other side, and no king, county, or town has any control over it."*

As the day was drawing to a close Colonel Leslie proposed that he be allowed to cross the bridge and pass a few yards beyond it and then he would turn around and cross back over it and leave. His orders were to cross the bridge, and he did not want to disobey orders. Both sides agreed to the conditions, and the drawbridge was lowered and the British quietly passed over it. Many of the town's people, however, were still angered by the appearance of the British in their town.

Near the bridge looking out of a window of a house was a nurse named Sarah Tarrant. She yelled out to the British troops, *"Go home and tell your master he has sent you on a fool's errand, and has broken the peace of our Sabbath; what do you think we were born in the woods, to be frighten by owls?"* [This was a common expression of the time that was meant to indicate that the speaker was use to danger and could not be easily frightened.]

This angered one of the British soldiers, so he raised his musket and aimed it at Sarah. Showing no fear she hollered at the soldier, *"Fire if you have the courage, but I doubt it."*

No one chose to do any firing that day, and Colonel Leslie and his men retreated back to their ship. Later, the Colonel was court martialed for his failure to perform his mission. Had the British soldier opened fire that day it could have resulted in firing on both sides. That would have resulted in the Revolutionary War starting in Salem and not in Concord and Lexington almost two months later.

Sources: 1. *A Glossary of Words & Phrases Usually Relating to the U.S.* by John Russell Bartlett, 1860. 2. *Account of Leslie's Retreat at the North Bridge in Salem* by Charles M. Endicott, 1856.

13 Was Always Unlucky For Me

James Miller may hold the record of the number of times a patriot was shot during battle. On April 19, 1775 the British were marching back to Boston after the battles of Lexington and Concord. As they marched back they were constantly shot at by American minutemen hiding behind rocks, fences, trees, and buildings. Outside of Cambridge at Prospect Hill the Americans fired a few rounds at the British and then retreated. James Miller, about sixty-six years old, and a companion had been firing at the British when the companion turned to James and said, *"Come on Miller, we've got to go."*

Miller answered back, *"I'm too old to run,"* so he remained and kept firing at the British. After the British had marched by the Americans found Miller dead and shot thirteen times.

Sources: 1. D.A.R. Lineage Book, Vol. 7, page 65. 2. *The Battle of April 19, 1775, in Lexington, Concord, Lincoln, Arlington, Cambridge, Somerville and Charlestown* by Frank Warren Coburn, 1912.

Now Is a Colonel Higher than a Captain?

Samuel Pierce received a Captain's commission from King George II and a Colonel's commission from the Continental Congress on the same day. He accepted the commission with the American army and served with distinction until the end of the war.

Source; 1. D.A.R. Lineage Book, Vol. 2, Page 47.

I Only Gave Him One Whack

The American Revolution began with the battles at Lexington and Concord on April 19, 1775. The first reported atrocity of the day occurred at Concord. When a group of British soldiers under the command of Captain Parsons were marching back to the North Bridge they noticed that one dead British soldier at the bridge had a savage cut to the head done by a hatchet.

Earlier in the day after the Americans and British had clashed at the North Bridge, both sides withdrew. After the firing [according to tradition] a young boy, Ammi White, was chopping wood for a clergyman, and after the battle he went with his axe in hand to the area. He found a wounded British soldier, and as the man tried to rise the boy used his axe to kill him. Later both sides condemned the action and the young boy regretted it the rest of his life.

Rumors began to quickly spread and the British later said that the Americans had scalped and cut the ears off their enemies. Mrs. Hulton, a supporter of the British, wrote in a letter in April of 1775, *"two or three of their people (British) lying with agonies of death scalped and their noses cut off and eyes bored out..."* Over time the number of men this happen to had grown to several.

As late as 1841 a British historian says, *"several were scalped, or had their ears cut off, by the Americans."*

A British officer who took part in the skirmish at Lexington described the event in a letter to the Massachusetts Governor shortly after the battle: *"While at Concord we saw vast numbers assembling in many parts; at one of the bridges they marched down, with a very considerable body, on the light infantry posted there. On their coming pretty near, one of our men fired on them, which they returned; on which an action ensued, and some few were killed and wounded. In this affair, it appears that after the bridge was quitted, they scalped and otherwise ill-treated one or two of the men who were either killed or severely wounded, being seen by a party that marched by soon after."*

Sources: 1. *Paul Revere's Ride* by David Fischer. 2. Battle Road: Birthplace of the American Revolution by Maurice R. Cullen. 3. President of the New England Historical Society, article: Antique News of Boston, Rev. Porter, pages 234-238.

Minutewomen

In the spring of 1775 Prudence Cummings Wright was thirty five years old and the mother of seven children. She lived with her husband David in Pepperell, Massachusetts. The British government considered Massachusetts the most rebellious of the thirteen colonies. There was no standing army in Massachusetts at this time, but what they did have were citizen soldiers called Minutemen.

These Minutemen had a network of messengers and signals that could alert the towns of any danger approaching them. When the men went off to fight, their wives remained behind and did their part such as molding bullets, gathering supplies, and tending to the chores at home. In some cases they also got involved as soldiers.

Early in the morning of April 19, 1775 news reached the home of David and Prudence Wright that the redcoats and patriots had fought at Lexington. They also learned that the British were now advancing toward Concord. The colonel of the local militia alerted the men of Pepperell to meet him at Groton a little over five miles away. The men grabbed their muskets, powder horns, a few supplies, and kissed their families good-by not knowing if they would return.

While her husband was with the Minutemen, Prudence was visiting her mother in Hollis, New Hampshire almost six miles away. While there she overheard some local Tories, who were friendly to the British, discussing plans to send messages between the British in the north and the British in Boston. She realized that the road the Tories would take between the north and Boston passed through the town of Pepperell.

The men of Pepperell were harassing the British troops as they marched back to the safety of Boston, so Prudence realized that it would be up to the women to stop the Tories from sending messages. Prudence returned to Pepperell and called to arms the thirty to forty women remaining in town. The women dressed in their men's clothing and gathered weapons, and they elected Prudence as the commander of their militia company. Prudence chose seventeen year old Sarah Hartwell Shattuck as her lieutenant and the newly formed company stood ready for a fight armed with muskets, pitchforks, and any other tool that could be used as a weapon.

The women gathered at the bridge over the Nashua River which was just outside of Pepperell on the road to Hollis. The women guarded the bridge, patrolled the road, and swore that no foe to freedom should pass that bridge. The company of women, who later became known as the Prudence Wright Guard, hoped that if British troops showed up they could scare the troops off before it was discovered that the patriots facing them were women.

The bridge was located out in the country with no homes nearby. The road to the bridge curved around an area of high ground, so that the bridge could not be seen until you were nearly on it if you were traveling from the north. The women waited all night in silence waiting for the enemy. Late in the night two riders approached the bridge, and Prudence jumped out in front of them and shone her lantern into their eyes. She demanded to know who they were and at what business they were on. When the startled men tried to escape, the company of women surrounded them and grabbed the reins of the horses.

One rider, Captain Leonard Whiting, was a well know Tory in the area and drew his pistol and was about to fire it. The other rider, also a Tory, was Samuel Cummings who was the brother of Prudence. Samuel told the captain to lower his weapon, when he recognized his sister's voice. He told the captain that his sister, *"would wade through blood for the rebel cause."* The two men dismounted, and when they were searched dispatches from the British troops in the north to the British in Boston were found in Samuel's boot. The prisoners were taken to a local home and guarded the rest of the night.

In the morning the women took their prisoners to Groton and turned them over to the Committee of Safety. The documents found on them were sent on to Charlestown. The two prisoners were later released on the condition that they never return to Massachusetts. Some versions of this story indicate that it was the other brother of Prudence, Thomas, rather than Samuel who was captured. Both of her brothers were Tories, and they left the area never to be seen by the family again. On March 19, 1777 town officials voted to award the women at the bridge seven pounds, seventeen shillings, and six pence for their services during the war.

Sources: 1. *Memorials of the Descendants of William Shattuck,* by Lemuel Shattuck, 1855, pages 330-331. 2. D.A.R. Lineage Book, Vol. 7, page 326. 3. *History in the Making, California State University, San Bernardino Journal of History, Vol. 9.* 4. *An Encyclopedia of American Women at War: from the Home Front to the Battlefield,* pages 668-69.

Never Too Old to Fight

On April 19, 1775 British forces were marching back to Boston following the battles of Lexington and Concord. As they marched toward the farm of Samuel Whittemore, they were about to encounter what may well be the oldest American soldier they would ever face.

Samuel was seventy-eight, according to some historians he may have been a few years older, and he was no stranger to soldiering. He fought in King George's War in 1745 as a member of the British Royal Dragoons. Samuel and his wife lived with their son and grandchildren on a farm in Menotomy, Massachusetts. Early in the morning the family was awakened when the British marched through their town on the way to Lexington and Concord. That afternoon Samuel was out working in the fields, when he heard gunfire as the returning British entered the town of Menotomy again.

Samuel, who was crippled, limped back to his house and gathered his weapons. His family was stunned as they watched him load his musket and both of his dueling pistols. He put powder and ball in his old worn military knapsack from the war of 1745. He then strapped his French made saber around his large waist and started walking toward the door.

His family begged him not to go, and one of the family members told him that the British would take him. Samuel told them that the British would find it hard work to do so. He then said, *"I'm going to fight some British regulars."*

He walked up, to what is today Massachusetts Street, to a secluded position behind a stone wall across the street from the church. Other patriots in the town were also firing at the British as they marched through town. Samuel waited patiently until about a dozen British troops were marching near him. He fired his musket, and then fired his two pistols killing one of the British soldiers and wounded two others. Samuel did not have time to re-load his weapons, so he drew his saber and began swinging it and cursing the Redcoats who had now surrounded him.

They overpowered the old man shooting him in the face, tearing half his cheek away, and knocking him down. Samuel tried to rise to continue the fight, but the British clubbed him with their musket butts and bayonetted him numerous times. Believing the old man was dead they continued their march.

After the British had left, the townspeople came out to retrieve the body of Samuel and were astonished that he was still alive. They used a door as a stretcher and carried the bloody body to Cooper's Tavern, which was serving as a hospital for the wounded. Doctor Cotton Tufts from Medford took a look at Samuel and said there was no use even dressing the wounds because he was going to die. At the insistence of some of Samuel's friends the doctor dressed the wounds and cleaned the body.

The next day in Boston an informant overheard some British soldiers talking about the fight on the road from Concord to Boston. One of the soldiers remarked, *"We killed an old devil there in Menotomy."* Another soldier added, *"But we paid most dear for it—lost three of our men, the last died this morning."* Samuel had the last laugh, because he survived and lived another eighteen years! It took several weeks before Samuel, due to the serious head wound, began to recognize family members. One asked him if he regretted his actions. Samuel said, *"No. I should do just so again."*

Sources: 1. *Peter's War: A New England Slave Boy and the American Revolution* by Joyce Lee Malcolm. 2. *Never Too Old: The Story of Captain Samuel Whittemore* by Donald N. Moran. 3. D.A.R. Lineage Book, Vol. 3, page 37. 4. *History of the Town of Arlington 1635-1879* by Benjamin and William Richard Cutter, 1898.

The Spirit of 1775

The following account is from a speech delivered in the House of Representatives of Massachusetts, February 3, 1851 by James T. Woodbury. He was requesting the town of Acton to build a monument over the remains of the three men that died on April 19, 1775.

James Hayward was a twenty-five year old schoolteacher who had no business answering the call to Concord. He had been excused from military service because he had a crippled foot due to an accident with an ax years earlier. No one would have thought ill of him if he had stayed home the morning of April 19, 1775, but he felt it his duty to answer the alarm. Since he was not a member of the company of minutemen he was not issued cartridges of powder and ball. Instead he carried loose powder in a powder horn.

After fighting at Concord, James with the other men, chased after the British down the road while they were retreating. He reached the house of Ebenezer Fiske's in Lexington and, probably due to his handicap, he stopped on the side of the road to rest. The British column had already passed so he was not concerned.

Two British regulars emerged from the farm house and approached James. One of the men pointed his musket at the boy and said, *"You're a dead man."* James grabbed his musket and replied, *"So are you."* Both men fired at the same time. The British soldier fell dead. James was shot through the side and survived another very painful eight hours.

James was eventually found by his father Samuel Hayward, who told the boy that the wound was fatal and did he regret answering the alarm. James weakly said, *"Father, hand me my powder horn and bullet pouch. I started with one pound of powder and forty balls, you see what I have left, you see what I have been about. I never did such a forenoon's work before. Tell mother not to mourn too much for me for I am not sorry I turned out. I die willingly for my country. She will now, I doubt not, by the help of God, be free. And tell whom I loved better than my mother, you know who I mean, that I am not sorry. I shall never see her again. May I meet her in heaven."*

Note: This author wonders if the story of the death of James Hayward is factual or simply the embellishment of a man hoping to encourage some politicians to give some money for a worthy cause. If the story is not true, then it should be, because it typified the spirt of many of the patriots that fought that day.

Source: 1. James T. Woodbury, Speech delivered in the House of Representatives of Massachusetts, February 3, 1851 upon the question of granting two thousand dollars to aid the town of Acton in building a monument over the remains of Capt. Isaac Davis, Abner Hosmer, and Jas. Hayward, Acton Minute Men, killed at Concord fight, April 19, 1775, (1851), page 38.

Old Woman Bags British Soldiers

West Cambridge has the honor of making the first capture of provisions and British prisoners of the American Revolution. On April 19, 1775 about 700 British troops under the command of Lieutenant Colonel Francis Smith were sent to Lexington and Concord, in order to capture and destroy rebel supplies that had been stored by the militia. British General Gage believed that reinforcements might be required to assist Colonel Smith. He order several regiments under the command of Earl Percy to leave Boston and march toward Colonel Smith.

Following in the rear of Percy's troops was a group of supply wagons that were having trouble crossing the Brighton Bridge. Word reached the rebels further ahead at Cooper's Tavern about the supply wagons and the rebels began making plans to capture them.

David Lampson, a free black man, told the following story to Colonel Thomas Russell who told it to Samuel Abbot Smith who wrote about it in his book, *"Meanwhile an express was sent post-haste from Old Cambridge to Menotomy, bearing the information that these supplies were on the way. Several of our men met at once in Cooper's tavern, which stood on the present site of Whittemore's hotel, to form some plan for capturing them. They were of the exempts, or alarm list as it was called, all old men, for every young man was that day nearer the post of danger. There were Jason Belknap and Joe Belknap, James Budge, Israel Mead and Ammi Cutter, David Lampson, and others, in all twelve. Some of them had been soldiers in the French war, and age had not impaired their courage. They chose for their leader David Lampson, a mulatto, who had served in the war, a man of undoubted bravery and determination."*

The twelve men took a position behind a wall of earth and stones and waited for the groups of wagons. *"The convoy soon made its appearance. As it came between them and the meeting house of the First Parish, Lampson ordered his men to rise and aim directly at the horses, and called out to them to surrender. No reply was made, but the drivers whipped up their teams. Lampson's men then fired, killing several of the horses, and, according to some accounts, killing two of the men and wounding others."*

Once the firing began, the drivers jumped from their wagons and ran to the bank of Spy Pond. They threw their guns into the pond and then continued to run along the banks of the pond. They followed along the bank and met an old woman named Mother Batherick.

"They surrendered themselves to mother Batherick who was digging dandelions. She led them to the house of Capt. Ephraim Frost, where there was a party of our men, saying to her prisoners, as she gave them up. 'If you ever live to get back, you tell King George that an old woman took six of his grenadiers prisoner.'"

The following made the rounds in some of the British newspapers. *"If one old Yankee woman can take six grenadiers, How many will be required to conquer America?"*

Source: 1. *West Cambridge 1775* by Samuel Abbot Smith, 1804, pages 26-31.

Payback

On April 19, 1775 as the British regulars under General Percy marched out of Boston toward Lexington and Concord, they played "Yankee Doodle Dandy" to taunt the Americans along the way. When the defeated British troops marched backed to Boston, they were taunted by Americans playing the song "Yankee Doodle Dandy." According to the May 20, 1775, "*Massachusetts Spy,*" newspaper upon their return to Boston one soldier asked his brother officer how he liked the tune now—"*Damn them!*" he replied, *"They made us dance it till we were tired."*

Source: 1. *Yankee Doodle and the Country Dance from Lexington to Yorktown* by Raymond F. Dolle.

Reuben Has Three Lives

Reuben Eaton left the town of Reading on April 19, 1775 and waited for the British after the battles of Lexington and Concord. He found the British a little past Meriam's Corner outside of Concord, so he hid behind a wall. As they approached he took deliberate and careful aim and fired at them. He later said about the adventure, *"O, it was glorious picking!"*

One time during the fight Reuben is almost picked off himself. He stayed at his firing place too long, and some British soldiers approached very close to him. Reuben started to run, and the soldiers immediately fired at him. Reuben dropped to the ground, although he was not hit. Thinking they killed him, the soldiers moved on. Reuben then jumped up and started running again, and once more the musket balls came flying by him. Again he dropped down on the ground like he was dead. After a minute or two Reuben jumped up and started to run. The troops saw him and fired, but he got away unhurt. He did hear one soldier say, *"See that Yankee; we have killed him twice, and look, he can run yet!"*

Sources: 1. Lineage Book, D.A.R. Vol. 51, page 134. 2. *Genealogical History of the Town of Reading, Mass.* by Hon. Lilley Eaton, 1874.

Just a Bunch of Boys Having Fun

On May 1, 1775 the students at Harvard were dismissed for an early summer vacation. They were told that when classes resumed on October 2nd they would be held at Concord twenty miles away. The newly formed colonial army was quartered in the school buildings during the winter of 1775-76.

When the soldiers left in the spring of 1776, they left behind damaged buildings. They tore off most of the roof of Harvard Hall and took the 1,000 pounds of metal to melt into bullets. They also stripped brass doorknobs and box locks from the buildings to melt into bullets. They even removed some interior woodwork to use as firewood. In 1778 Harvard petitioned the Massachusetts' government to pay for the damage, and they were awarded the sum of 417 pounds.

Source: 1. Ireland, Corydon, Harvard's Year of Exile, Harvard Gazette, 13 October, 2011.

Which Declared First?

On May 18, 1775 elected officials of Mecklenburg County met at a courthouse in Charlotte, North Carolina to discuss the problems that were brewing with Great Britain. On that day an express rider arrived with news of the British attack on Lexington and Concord. Overcome with feelings of patriotism the delegates drew up five revolutionary measures.

The most incendiary of these stated, *"That we the citizens of Mecklenburg County, do hereby dissolve the political bands which have connected us to the Mother Country, and...declare ourselves a free and independent people..."* These five statements were called the Mecklenburg Declaration of Independence. This would have occurred a year before the Declaration of Independence by the thirteen colonies.

Most historians believe that the Mecklenburg Declaration was nothing more than a document called the Mecklenburg Resolves. These resolves were resolutions that did not mention an actual declaration of independence, but rather they only suspended British civil and military influence until the King addressed colonial grievances.

The document that claimed independence from Great Britain was supposedly destroyed in a fire in 1800. This means there is no proof that it ever existed. The Mecklenburg Resolves do exist, because they were published in a newspaper in 1775. So the question remains, did North Carolina declare independence a year before the colonies or not?

Sources: 1. *That Other Declaration: May 20, 1775* by Richard M. Current, North Carolina Historical Review page 54, pages 161-191. 2. *The Mecklenburg Declaration of Independence: A Study of Evidence Showing that the Alleged Early Declaration of Independence is Spurious* by William Henry Hoyt, 1907.

Fighting to be Free in Your Own Country

Samuel Ashbow was one of four brothers who fought in the American Revolution. He was one of at least thirty Mohegan Native Americans who served in the war and many served on privateer ships. Samuel was born in Connecticut around 1746, and after the battles at Concord and Lexington he and his brother John fought at Breed's Hill (usually called the Battle of Bunker Hill) on June 16, 1775.

The two brothers were stationed at a rail fence on the Northside of the hill with the rest of the Connecticut troops. These troops held the British back on the first two attacks, However, they were overtaken on the third attack. It may have been during this attack that Samuel became the first Native American to die in the American Revolution. He is buried on Breed's Hill in a mass grave with many other Americans that died that day. His brother Robert died in 1776 during the retreat from New York.

Sources: 1. *Patriots of Color; African Americans and Native Americans at Battle Road & Bunker Hill* by George Quintal Jr. 2. *Fourth of July Celebrations Lost to History* by Bill Stanley, Norwich Bulletin, January 29, 2008.

It Never Occurred to Me that He Would Ride Away

Cuff Whittemore was a slave that belonged to William Whittemore in Cambridge, Massachusetts. On June 4, 1775 he was allowed to enlist, probably in place of his owner, for eight months in Colonel Thomas Gardner's Regiment. At the Battle of Bunker Hill Cuff fought bravely and was wounded. As he retreated with the other patriots, he seized a British sword from a slain officer.

In May 1777 Cuff reenlisted in the Continental Army for three years and served in Colonel William Shepard's Regiment. Cuff fought at Saratoga and was taken prisoner, and while in the British camp he was ordered to take care of General Burgoyne's horse.

One morning, just before the capture of British General Burgoyne, Cuff was told to take the General's favorite horse to the brook for water. On the other side of the brook about a half a mile away was the American army. After the horse drank its fill, Cuff jumped on the back of the horse and road toward the American lines. As British bullets flew by him, he rode off and rejoined the American army.

After the war Cuff received a pension for his service, and when he died in Charlestown, Massachusetts on January 26, 1826 he was one of a very few men of color to be honored with an obituary notice. The notice was published in *Columbian Sentinel: "In Charlestown Mr. Cuff Whittemore age 75 a soldier of the revolutionary war and a man of color."*

Source: 1. *Biographies of Patriots of Color at the Battle of Bunker Hill.*

But I Have This Nice Uniform at Home

After the battles of Lexington and Concord the Americans had an army of militia men that needed a commander. Congress met and began to consider who should lead the army. John Hancock expected that the Second Congress would name him the Commander-in-Chief. He would then be able to wear the gorgeous uniform he had custom made for himself and lead the troops into battle against the British. This war with England would also free him from the hundreds of indictments for smuggling that were pressing in the courts. John Hancock was disappointed when John Adams nominated George Washington to the post, and he was accepted unanimously. Washington assumed command of the continental Army in Cambridge on July 3, 1775.

Source: 1. *Washington: A Life* by Ron Chernow.

Don't Pay Me, Just Grant me a Few Necessities

When George Washington was appointed Commander-in Chief of the Continental Army, he refused to accept the $500 a month pay for the position. Instead, he offered to only accept his expenses as his pay. He wrote to Congress, *"Sir, I beg leave to assure the Congress that as no pecuniary consideration could have tempted me to have accepted this arduous employment, I do not wish to make any profit from it. I will keep an exact account of my expenses. Those I doubt not they will discharge, and that is all I desire."*

After eight years he turned in his personal expense account to Congress which was a bill for $160,074. His total expenses, which included his personal expense account and money spent on the members of his headquarters, or his military family as he called them, came to a whopping $449,261.51.

Washington was an aristocrat land owner and was used to the finer things, even in war. The final bill included such personal items as a saddle and case. Washington wrote an accounting entry on June 22, 1775, *"To cash paid for Sadlery, a Letter Case, Maps, Glasses, &c &c &c. for the use of my Command... $831.45."* From July 21-22 1775 he bought *"a pig, a number of ducks, 1 dozen pigeons, veal, 1 dozen squash, 2 dozen eggs, hurtleberries, biscuit and a cork cask."*

Washington's expenses for July 4, 1776 included a broom (which cost 6 pence) as well as mutton, veal, beef, cabbage, beets, beans, potatoes, and lobster. He also paid for the mending of his "Chariot" a type of carriage. From September 1775 to March 1776 Washington spent over $6,000 on alcohol to entertain various visitors. After the war Congress approved his expenses.

Source: 1. National Archives RG 56, General Records, Treasury Department.

You Must be Kidding! You Call This an Army?

When General George Washington took command of the newly formed Continental Army on July 3, 1775 in Cambridge, he was not aware of the sad state of the troops. Later in September he wrote that the true conditions of the troops were not what he was led to believe. So exactly what did the General find on his first day?

The troops were a mixture of farmers and shop keepers with little military training. Some had served in the French and Indian War that was fought years earlier. For most men experiences with muskets consisted of hunting animals for food. They came from various small towns across the area, and they did not agree on the same rules of conduct. Their officers were selected by vote and were usually the leading citizens of the town. The army was supplemented by local militias, who would usually serve for a short time and then go back home. Washington described his men as *"a mixed multitude of people under very little discipline, order, or government."*

His army lived in makeshift huts, their uniforms were whatever they wore from home, and their weapons consisted of the family muskets. He later discovered that the amount of powder in camp and the surrounding area amounted to about nine rounds per man. Most of the men were more worried about their crops at home than they were about fighting the British. Washington was shocked that the enlisted men and their officers treated each other as equals. He even saw officers shaving the enlisted men. He found some of the men engaging in conversations with the British across the lines.

To make matters worse the men considered Washington as an outsider. After all, he was a wealthy land owner from Virginia, and most of them were working class men from New England. A week after he arrived Washington wrote to his friend Richard Henry Lee, *"I think we are in an exceedingly dangerous situation, as our numbers are not much larger than we suppose those of the enemy to be."*

On his first day of arrival Washington began to issue general orders on establishing order and obedience. To disobey the orders invited swift and harsh punishment. He later wrote, *"Discipline is the soul of an army. It makes small numbers formidable; procures success to the weak and esteem to all."*

Sources: 1. *Life of Washington; A Biography* by Benson J. Lossing, pages 593-598. 2. *Life and Times of Washington* by Schroeder-Lossing, pages 792-796. 3. *The Writings of George Washington* by Jared Sparks, pages 486-490. 3. Letter to John Augustine Washington, July 27, 1775, National Archives. 4. Artemas Ward orderly book, pages 3-8, July 1775, National Archives.

Bon Appétit

When Colonel Benedict Arnold invaded Canada in the summer of 1775, Pastor Samuel Spring agreed to serve as a chaplain of the expedition. That winter food became very scarce, and the men began to eat anything they could find. One day Pastor Spring came upon a company of men gathered around a fire, while boiling some dog's claws they had saved to make a soup with. They urged the pastor to sit with them and share the disgusting meal. When the dog gave out, the men took off their moose skin moccasins and boiled them to extract a little nourishment. They felt their feet could withstand the cold November mornings more than their stomachs could endure the hunger pangs.

Sources: 1. Sons of the American Revolution Application. 2. *From Its European Antecedents to 1791—The United States Army Chaplaincy* by Parker C. Thompson, 1978, pages, 122-4. 3. Blackstone Valley Tribune, Vol II, Number 10, 5 December, 2008, article by Michael Potaski, page 5. 4. *The Chaplains and Clergy of the Revolution by Joel Tyler Headly*, 1864, pages 89-106.

The Absent-Minded Code Breaker

Pastor Samuel West was extremely absent-minded, and he often forgot where he was going or why. Sometimes he was not even aware of events going on around him. Friends would at times find him sitting on his horse, as the horse was grazing on the side of the road. The bridle was loose, and Samuel would be sitting on the horse with his hands folded on his breast totally absorbed in his own thoughts.

One time he met a friend, and he said to the man that he and his wife were on their way to visit him. The friend asked him, *"Where is your wife?"* Samuel replied, *"Why, I thought she was on the seat behind me."* His wife was getting ready to join him, and Samuel had ridden off without her.

When General Washington had his headquarters at Cambridge, he learned that the British Admiral at Newport, Rhode Island had received secrets of American civil and military affairs. Finally, a cypher letter was found by Washington, which indicated that it was written by someone on his own staff. Washington's trusted men could find no one to decipher the letter, until someone said there was a chaplain with troops at Dorchester who might be able to read it. They summoned

Chaplain Samuel West to crack the code in the letter. Washington also had two other code breakers called in, Elbridge Gerry and Colonel Elisha Porter. Washington had Gerry and Porter to work as a team and Samuel to work alone. The General wanted to see if each group would decipher the same hidden message.

A tent was prepared for Samuel, and a detail was assigned to guard his quarters while he worked at the message. The pastor began his study of the coded message as soon as lights out was shouted by the sentries. Samuel worked through the night, and by daybreak he sent word to headquarters that he was ready to reveal the contents of the letter and who wrote it.

The code used in the letter was known as a "monalphabetic substitution" where one letter or in this case a symbol was substituted for a letter of the alphabet. Fortunately, for the Americans it was one of the easiest codes to break. In the English language some letters are consistently used more frequently than others. An example of a simple type of substitution:

Plain text alphabet: A B C D E F G H I J K L M N O P Q R S T U V W X Y Z

Ciphertext alphabet: Z E B R A S C D FG H I J K LM NO P Q T U V W X Y

American soldiers are here! (uncoded message) plain text alphabet

Zjaolgbzq plrfaop zoa daoa! (the coded message) cipher text alphabet

Washington received the coded message from the team of Porter and Gerry and the one from Samuel. When he compared the two messages they were identical. The coded letter revealed American casualties, troop strength, the mood of the people in many of the towns, and shipments of gunpowder. The original cipher letter was sent to Major Cane, a British officer in Boston, through a former mistress. After questioning the woman she admitted that the sender of the letter was Doctor Benjamin Church, who was serving as the Chief Physician and Director General of Medical Service of the Continental Army.

On October 3, 1775 Church was taken before a court of inquiry with General Washington presiding. Church was visibly shaken when the court showed him the decoded message. He admitted he sent it, and he tried to defend his actions by saying that he sent exaggerated accounts of weapons and supplies to convince the British that to continue the war was a mistake. The court was not impressed with his story, and found him guilty of criminal action, and referred to the Continental Congress for its action.

Church was found guilty by Congress and could have been executed except for a loophole. The Congress had approved on November 7, 1775 to allow the death penalty for convicted spies, but because Church was convicted of spying before the death penalty had been authorized, it did not apply to him. Dr. Church was sent to jail in Norwich, Connecticut and remained under guard until 1778. He was then banished and sailed from Boston, presumably for Martinique, and he was never heard from again. It was believed that the ship he was on was lost at sea.

Sources: 1. *A History of the Town of Acushnet, Bristol County, State of Massachusetts* by Franklin Howland, page 78. 2. *The Writings of George Washington* by Jared Sparks, 1837, pages 504-6. 3. *The Original American Spies: Seven Covert Agents of the Revolutionary War* by Paul R. Misencik, pages 41-5. 4. Harvard Alumni Veterans of the American Revolutionary War.

The Impossible Will take Just a Little Longer

One of the most remarkable feats during the Revolution occurred during the winter of 1775. The Americans had laid siege to Boston and had fought the Battles of Lexington and Concord. The bookstore in Boston owned by Henry Knox had been looted and his stock destroyed, when the British were surrounded by the Americans in April of 1775. Henry snuck out of Boston with his wife and joined the American militia. He used his engineering skills to help fortify the American positions around Boston. When Washington took command of the army in July, he was impressed with the work that Knox had done.

There appeared little chance of breaking the siege and driving the British out of Boston without using siege guns. These heavy guns were needed, because they had the range to throw shots at the British in the town. Colonel Knox approached General Washington with plan to haul sixty tons of cannons over 300 miles, in the dead of winter, across ice covered rivers, and over snow blanketed mountains to the American camp outside of Boston. These large guns had been captured at Fort Ticonderoga in upstate New York and were just sitting there.

It took Knox and his men from December 5 to January 27 to haul the equipment by ox-drawn sleds. The cannons were then deployed, and on March 2 they began to bombard the British. Once the sailing winds became favorable, the British left Boston on March 15.

On December 23, 1776 George Washington had Knox appointed Brigadier General of Artillery. Washington Irving wrote about Knox in his book *Life of Washington*, *"Knox was one of those providential characters which spring up in emergencies, as if they were formed by and for the occasion."*

Sources: 1. *Memories of Henry Knox,* Joseph W. Porter, editor, pages 3-4. 2. *Henry Knox A Soldier of the Revolution* by Noah Brooks, pages 38-43. 3. *Life and Correspondence of Henry Knox* by Francis S. Drake, pages 22-24.

We Will Overlook Your Destruction of the Bridge This Time

William "Billy" Flora was a free-born African American from Virginia who served as a soldier in the revolution. In the American victory at the Battle of Great Bridge in December of 1775 Billy played a very important role. Billy took up a plank on the bridge that prevented the British from crossing the bridge. His commander Captain Thomas Nash wrote, *"Flora, a colored man, was the last sentinel that came into the breastwork. He did not leave his post until he had fired several times. Billy had to cross a plank to get to the breastwork, and had fairly passed over it when he was seen to turn back, and deliberately take up the plank after him, amidst a shower of musket balls."*

Source: 1. *African Americans in the Revolutionary War* by Michael Lanning.

The Great Snowball Fight of 1775

In 1775 General George Washington had the task of molding men from different regions into a single American Army. On a snowy day in December of 1775 his work was in danger of unraveling.

American troops fortifying Cambridge during the Siege of Boston needed places to stay. The president of Harvard Samuel Langdon offered his campus to Washington's troops. The five Harvard buildings were used to house 1,600 troops during the winter months, and the Harvard students moved their studies to Concord. Tents and barracks were assembled in Harvard Yard for the troops.

The troops that first moved in were from New England such as the 27th Continental Regiment. One day in December a rifle corps from Virginia came into the American camp. The Virginia boys were mainly backwoods and mountain boys, and this was their first time to venture out of their communities. They acted different and dressed different from that of the regiments from New England.

The Virginia troops excited the curiosity of the troops from New England, particularly the Marblehead Regiment from Massachusetts. This regiment was composed of seafaring men who were always full of fun and mischief. The Marblehead boys wore heavy round jackets and loose fisherman trousers compared to the buckskins and white linen frocks with ruffles and fringe that the boys from Virginia wore. To make matters worse the Massachusetts troops had some black troops with them. The Virginia boys saw the blacks as slaves and not equals, which caused even more tension.

The two groups began making remarks about how silly the other group dressed. Soon the boys began to get serious with each other, and since there was snow on the ground they began throwing snowballs. In no time the playing developed into a heated battle with snowballs flying everywhere. In a matter of minutes the battle escalated with biting, hitting, and gouging. The yard quickly filled with hundreds of combatants engaged in hand-to-hand combat.

A ten year old boy, Israel Trask, was a witness to the event and wrote about what happened next, *"At this juncture General Washington made his appearance, whether accident of design I never knew. I only saw him and his colored servant, both mounted. With the spring of a deer he leaped from his saddle, three reins of his bridle into the hands of his servant and rushed into the thickest of the melee with an iron grip seized two, brawny, athletic, savage looking riflemen by the throat keeping them at arm's length alternately shaking and talking to them. In the position the eye of the belligerents caught sight of the General. Its effect on them was instantaneous flight at the top of their speed in all directions from the scene of conflict. Less than fifteen minutes time had lapsed from the commencement of the row before the general and his two criminals were the only occupants of the field of action."*

Most people would have thought that the General would have taken the two men and imprisoned them, court martialed them, and perhaps given them the lash. Instead, Washington released the men and left. The hostile feeling between the two groups ceased because of the mere presence of the physical and mental strength displayed by Washington. The fact that Washington grabbed two fellow Virginians showed the men that he would not be influenced by regional loyalties.

Sources: 1. Pension Application S30171 for Israel Trask. 2. *Harvard's Year of Exile*, Harvard Gazette by Corydon Ireland.

Chapter 3

"These are the times that try men's souls: The summer soldier and the sunshine patriot will, in this crisis, shrink from the service of his country; but he that stands it now, deserves the love and thanks of man and woman." Written by Thomas Paine in his pamphlet *American Crisis No. 1*. Read aloud to the Continental Army three days before the Battle of Trenton December 1776.

Dark Days of War in the Northern Colonies 1776-1777

The fate of the colonies did not look very promising at the start of 1776. The colonists faced problems on two fronts; political and military. The people were still divided about what they wanted from England. Did they just want to make a statement of grievances, or did they want complete independence? Could their rag-tag army hold out long enough to achieve either?

Military Front:

The newly formed Continental Army consisted of a few thousand men that were short of supplies, money, and hope. During the entire war about 231,000 would serve, and never more than 48,000 at any one time, and less than 13,000 men at any one place. Many of the additional soldiers were in militia units made up of ill-trained soldiers, who many times would turn and run at the first sight of the advancing British troops. At the start of 1776 General Washington had a force of less than 20,000 Continental soldiers.

Facing the American army were British General Howe's force of 32,000 men. Thousands of Tories and Native Americans joined the British forces. The King sent an additional force of 30,000 German Hessians, who were hired out by German princes to serve with the British troops.

On the sea the Americans faced even greater odds. At the start of 1776 Congress had authorized construction of thirteen new frigates. Only eight made it to sea, and their effectiveness was very limited. The new American navy faced over a hundred British ships of the line manned by 40,000 experienced sailors.

In 1776 the Americans faced many defeats on the battlefield, shortages of supplies, and problems keeping enlistments up within their army. By September the British had captured New York City, and Washington's army was in full retreat. The British now controlled much of New England.

Washington knew that he needed to gain a victory, or face the defeat of his army and the Revolution. Washington then devised a plan to cross the Delaware River on Christmas night and attack a garrison of Hessians at Trenton. The surprise attack was successful, and an excited Washington proclaimed, *"This is a glorious day for our country."* He had little time to celebrate, because by December 29 nearly half of his army of 2,400 men had gone home. The enlistments of the rest of the men would expire in the next couple of days. Washington needed a miracle, or the American army would disappear by the start of 1777. He appealed to his men to stay and fight for the cause of liberty. He also offered them a $10 bounty, which he was not authorized to do. By the end of the day over 1,200 men had reenlisted.

The year 1777 starts well for the Americans. After the victory at Trenton, more men enlist in the army and militia units. American forces defeat the British at Princeton and again at Trenton. For the next few months the British again overwhelm the American forces, and once more the cause of liberty is in jeopardy. With the American victory at Saratoga in the fall there is hope that the French and other nations will now support the Americans' fight for independence. The American army makes winter camp at Valley Forge and again faces disease, food shortages, and a shrinking army.

Political Front:

At the start of 1776 some colonists still held out hope that Americans could reconcile with the King of England. Support for declaring their independence began to grow, when it was discovered that King George had hired the despised German Hessians to fight against the Americans. It was believed that they would butcher American troops and spread terror among the civilian population.

Many of the leaders in the colonies began to call for independence to be declared. In January Thomas Paine published the pamphlet *Common Sense*, which made a case for independence. After a much heated debate Congress appointed a committee in June to draft a declaration. Once the declaration was presented there was more debate, changes made, and on July 4, 1776 the wording was approved, and the Declaration of Independence was sent to the printer. The colonies had officially severed political ties with Great Britain.

On October 26, 1776 Benjamin Franklin was sent to France by the Continental Congress to negotiate a formal alliance and treaty with France. The defeat of the British at Saratoga in October of 1777 convinced the French that the Americans might be able to defeat their enemy the British. The King of France ordered his officials to begin negotiations of an alliance with the Americans. The impossible had now become possible.

Think About What You Are About to Say

Medad Butler and several other boys educated their pastor about the revolution in 1776. The minister of the town church was a Loyalist and avoided giving any encouragement to the people to join the rebel cause. Several of the boys in town, including Medad, were very supportive of the patriot cause, and they decided they would try and change the attitude of the pastor.

One Saturday they got possession of a cannon, loaded it, and placed it at the rear of the church pointing toward the pulpit. All of this mischief was done at night and in silence. The next morning as the pastor was entering the church, the boys pointed out the cannon to him and what it was aimed at. They told the pastor that if he failed to pray for the success of the rebel cause, the cannon would be fired while he was at the pulpit. It was reported that while in church the pastor became a supporter of the rebel cause.

Sources: 1. Sons of the American Revolution Application. 2. D.A.R. Lineage Book, Vol. 17. 3. *The Life and Letters of Charles Butler* by Francis Hovery Stoddard.

The Strongest Man in the Revolution

Peter Francisco was born in 1760 and was believed to be the son of a wealthy Portuguese family. There are various stories about his arrival in North America, when he was four years old. He was found in 1765 on the wharf by dock workers in Virginia. He was taken to a poor house and later Judge Anthony Winston, the uncle of Patrick Henry, took the young boy in his home.

At the age of sixteen Peter, who was now six and a half feet tall and weighed over 260 pounds, joined the 10th Virginia Regiment. Because of his size and exploits on the battlefield he became known as the "Virginia Giant" or the "Virginia Hercules." It was said that, *"Francisco could take with his two arms two men weighing 160 pounds by their legs, and at arm's length raise them to the ceiling."*

He fought in numerous battles including Brandywine, Germantown, Monmouth, and Cowpens. At the Battle of Stony Point he suffered a nine inch gash in his stomach from a bayonet. Some writers claim that he was the second American to reach the inside of the British fort. There was never any proof of this feat. Many of the stories of Peter contain myth mixed with truth. He killed many British soldiers in these battles, and he was wounded many times.

His legend began at the Battle of Camden. The Americans were retreating and were forced to leave behind one of their cannons stuck in mud. According to the story which may or may not be true, Peter picked up the 1,100 pound cannon and carried it from the battlefield on his shoulder.

During the Battle of Guilford Courthouse he killed eleven British soldiers, before he received a bayonet wound in the leg. He killed the soldier that bayonetted him and continued to fight. He was later wounded severely and lay on the battlefield bleeding to death. A Quaker, who was searching for wounded, found him and took Peter back to his farm. He nursed him back to health, and Peter returned to his company.

Another story was told how he defeated a band of Tarleton's Raiders. In this action it was said he killed several British soldiers and escaped from the rest. It was reported that General Washington once referred to him as *"a one man army."*

Peter joined the army at Yorktown but did not fight. He did witness the surrender of the British army to the Americans. After the war he married, and later in life he became very poor. He died from appendicitis in 1831.

One story about his strength circulated after he left the army. A very strong man named Pamphlet came all the way from Kentucky to whip Peter. When Peter faced him, he handed Pamphlet some willow switches and told him to start whipping him. Pamphlet did not see the humor in the remark and asked Peter to let him feel how heavy he was.

He lifted Peter off the ground and said that he was quite heavy. Peter told Pamphlet it was his turn to feel the weight of his adversary. Peter lifted him off the ground twice, and on the third lift he threw him over a fence, which was four feet high, into a road. The amazed Pamphlet called out to Peter that it would be a great favor if Peter would also throw his horse after him, as he wanted to go home. The story goes on to say that Peter took the horse to the fence and threw him over as requested.

Sources: 1. Sons of the American Revolution Application. 2. *Daring Deeds of the Old Heroes of the Revolution by Henry C. Watson, 1893*, pages 160-162. 3. William and Mary College Quarterly Historical Magazine Vol. XIII, April, 1905, No. 4, pages 214-220.

It's Better to Hold Your Tongue Around Some People

George Ransom enlisted in 1776 at the age of fourteen as a private in Captain Samuel Ransom's Company. His first job with the unit was to bury the dead, and on January 20, 1777 he fought in his first battle at the Battle of Millstone. George fought at the Battle of Brandywine, Germantown, and he was also present for the Siege of Fort Mifflin. He celebrated his sixteenth birthday at Valley Forge with General George Washington.

In the summer of 1779 Spaulding's company, including George Ransom, joined the Sullivan Expedition and served as scouts. They were engaged at the Battle of Newtown on August 29, 1779. This American victory was against a combined force of Tories and Iroquois' warriors. It successfully ended the threat of the Indians in upper New York. More than forty Iroquois' villages were destroyed in the expedition. George later referred to this venture as *"bashing the Indians."*

Near the end of the war in December of 1780 George, who had been promoted to First Sergeant, returned to his home in Wyoming Valley. In December George visited the home of Benjamin Harvey, in order to court Benjamin's seventeen year old daughter Elisha. During the evening Indians raided the house and took the five occupants, including George, as captives. The next morning the Indians released two of the captives, but they kept George, Elisha, and Benjamin.

After several days, the Indians tied Benjamin to a tree and took turns throwing tomahawks at his head. The young braves missed every time, and the leader of the Indians thought that Benjamin must have been protected by the Great Spirit, so Benjamin was set free. They continued north with George and Elisha. George was later turned over to the British in Montreal and Elisha remained with the Indians through the winter. She was later traded to a Scotsman for a half barrel of rum. Two years later her father was able to get her released in a prisoner exchange, and she returned home.

In February of 1781 George was moved with other prisoners to Quebec to a place called Prison Island. The head guard was an eighteen year old Scottish soldier, who would at times order the men to shovel snow. If a prisoner refused they were chained in irons. When George and another prisoner, William Palmeters, were asked they refused. The two men were placed in an open floorless house overnight in freezing temperatures. The next morning George was asked again to shovel the snow. He replied, *"Not by order of a damned Tory!"* The two prisoners were chained again and moved to another building, and they were subjected to various abuses throughout the winter.

In early June, George and two other prisoners would at times sneak away during work detail and work on building a raft. On June 9th they escaped on the raft and crossed the St. Lawrence River. Exhausted and with little food, mainly eating captured snakes and frogs, they managed to reach Lake Champlain in two days. The men eventually reached the village of Putney, Vermont and split up. George walked south to Litchfield, Connecticut where he was born. The other two men walked to Albany, New York. After George regained his health he rejoined the 1st Connecticut militia and remained with them until he was discharged at West Point in 1783. George's military background proved that he is a tough man and would not back down from a fight.

When George was an old man he overheard a young man criticize General Washington. Enraged, George took his cane and knocked the man down. George was taken to court and was questioned by Judge Hollenback. The judge asked the old man where he was in 1777, in July of 1778, in the summer of 1779, and in the winter of 1780. George said he was in Washington's army, heading back to Wyoming Valley to bury his father, with General Sullivan, and a prisoner on the St. Lawrence. The judge then asked him, *"And did you knock the fellow down, Colonel Ransom?"* *"I did so, and would do it again under like provocation,"* said the Colonel defiantly. *"What was the provocation?"* George responded, *"The rascal abused the name of General Washington."*

Judge Hollenback had heard enough evidence and fined George Ransom one penny and ordered the young man to pay the court costs. The people in the court room applauded.

Sources: 1. Sons of the American Revolution Application. 2. *Register of the Pennsylvania Society of the Sons of the Revolution, 1888-1898* by Ethan Allen Weaver. 3. Pension Papers W2694 of George Ransom. 4. *History of Westmoreland County, Pennsylvania, Vol. 1* by John Newton Boucher. 5. *A Genealogical Record of the Descendants of Captain Samuel Ransom of the Continental Army* by Captain Clinton B. Sears, 1882. 6. *New England Families, Genealogical and Memorial, Vol 2*, edited by William Richard Cutter.

I Would Rather Face Death in Battle than Face My Father

In February of 1776 Hugh McDonald's father, a Tory, took him along with him to the Battle of Moore's Creek. Both were taken prisoner by the rebel militia, and they were both set free to return home. That June Hugh and his father were working in their field, when they heard rebel horsemen approaching. Hugh's father hid, and the rebel officers ordered Hugh to guide them through the settlement. Hugh refused and claimed that if he did his father would kill him. The rebels forced him to go with them and later released him. Once released, Hugh who was fearful of his father refused to go home. He decided to join the rebel army, and he sought out an officer that he knew and trusted.

Hugh McDonald wrote in the form of a journal his experiences in the American Revolution. The following are excerpts from his journal, which are found in the North Carolina University Magazine of December 1853. This excerpt tells how he came to join the American army.

"Notwithstanding this scouring," at Moore's Creek, *"and the just contempt of our fellow citizens, we remained in heart as still tories as ever. This expedition took place in the month of February, 1776, from which we returned and began to repair our fences for a crop the ensuing summer. About the first of June, a report was circulated that a company of lighthorse were coming into the settlement; and, as a guilty conscience needs no accuser, every one thought they were after him. The report was that Col. Alston had sent out four or five men to cite us all to muster at Henry Eagle's, on Bear Creek, upon which our poor deluded people took refuge in the swamps. On a certain day, when we were ploughing in the field, news came to my father that the light horse were in the settlement and a request that he would conceal himself. He went to the house of his brother-in-law to give him notice, and ordered me to take the horse out of the plough, turn him loose, and follow him as fast as I could. I went to the horse, but never having ploughed any in my life, I was trying how I could plough, when five men on horseback appeared at the fence, one of whom, Dan'l Buie, knew me and asked me what I was doing here. I answered that my father lived here; and he said he was not aware of that. 'Come,' he says, you must go with us to pilot us through the settlement; for we have a boy here with us who has come far enough. He is six miles from home and is tired enough.—' His name was Thomas Graham, and he lived near the head of McLennon's creek. I told Mr. Buie that I dare not go, for, if I did, my father would kill me.*

He then alighted from his horse, and walked into the field, ungeared the horse and took him outside the fence." "He then put up the fence again; and, leading me by the hand, put me on behind one of the company, whose name was Gaster, and discharged the other boy. We then went to Daniel Shaw's, thence to John Morrison's (shoemaker), thence to Alexander McLeod's, father of merchant John McLeod, who died in Fayetteville, thence to Alexander Shaw's, (blacksmith), thence to old Hugh McSwan's, who gave half a crown for a small gourd when we landed in America. Here I was ordered to go home, but I refused, and went with them to the muster at Eagle's. Next day Col. Phillip Alston appeared at the muster, when these men told him that they had taken a boy to pilot them a little way through the settlement and that they could not get clear of him. The Colonel personally insisted on my going back to my father; but I told them I would not; for I had told them the consequence of my going with them before they took me. Seeing he could not prevail with me, he got a man by the name of Daniel McQueen, a noted bard, to take me home to my father, but I told him that I was determined to hang to them. Col. Alston then took me with him and treated me kindly. Mrs. Alston desired me to go to school with her children until she could send my father word to come after me, and she would make peace between us; but her friendly offers were also rejected."

"On the following Tuesday I went with the same company of horsemen to Fayetteville, where I met a gentleman by the name of Dan'l. Porterfield, a Lieutenant in Capt. Authur Council's company, who asked me if I did not wish to enlist. I told him, not with him; but I wanted to see a Mr. Hilton who, I understood, was in the army, and wherever he was I wished to be. He told me that he and Hilton were of one company, and if Hilton did not tell me so, he would take back the money and let me go with Hilton. I then took the money and was received into the service of the U. S. June 10th, 1776, and in the fourteenth year of my age."

Hugh was at Valley Forge and served in many battles, and later he received a pension for his service.

Sources: 1. North Carolina and Tennessee Revolutionary War Land Warrants. 2. Pension Papers S41837 & W8438. 3. U.S. Pensioners 1818-1872. 4. Roster of Known Soldiers of the 6th Regiment North Caroline Line. 5. *Becoming*

Men of Some Consequence: Youth and Military Service in the Revolutionary War by John A. Ruddiman. 6. *Memoir by Hugh McDonald* (extract) North Carolina University Magazine, December 1853, Vol. 11, pages 828-837.

Don't Take a Broadsword to a Musket Fight, Laddie

The Battle of Moore's Creek was fought February 27, 1776. The American militia consisted of about 800 men, and they made fortifications on the east side of Moore's Bridge. A large band of Tories showed up numbering about 800, of which 600 were Scots.

Just before dawn eighty of the Tory Scots waving Scottish Claymore broadswords prematurely charged across the bridge. Scottish pipes were blaring and drums were beating, and the Scots yelled, *"King George and broadswords."* They were not aware that the patriots were waiting behind fortifications with their muskets aimed at them. At least thirty of the Tories were killed, and it was reported that McLeod, the leader of the charge, had been struck by at least twenty musket balls. Only one patriot was killed, reported to be John Grady, in the rebel victory.

Sources: 1. *The American Revolution in the Southern Colonies* by David Lee Russell. 2. Pension Papers S34132. 3. *A Guide to the Battles of the American Revolution* by Theodore P. Savas and J. David Dameron.

The Family that Fights Together Stays Together

John Guyer wrote in his pension application, *"I enlisted as a drummer for the term of twenty-one months, in the month of March in the year 1776 near Pittsburg in the company commanded by Captain Irwin in the regiment commanded by Colonel Miles in the line in the state of Pennsylvania."*

John enlisted at the age of eleven, and his father Peter also enlisted in the 13th Pennsylvania State Rifle Regiment in Captain Irwin's Company under the command of Colonel Samuel Miles.

Mary, the mother of John, accompanied them as a wash woman for the company. The family served for twenty-one months and were present at the battles of Fort Washington, Trenton, Princeton, Brandywine, and Germantown. At the Battle of Germantown Peter was wounded in the groin by a bayonet and shot in the leg. John was shot in the heel.

Unfortunately, Washington's army would have to spend the harsh winter at Valley Forge. With John and Peter wounded and food and supplies scarce, it must have been a difficult march to Valley Forge. Due to Peter's two wounds, he was discharged and the family made the 140 mile trip back to their home.

Sources: 1. *Book of American Revolutionary Soldiers, Archives 5th Ser. Vol 2.* 2. *Revolutionary War Rolls in Penn. 1775-1778.* 3. Pension application for John Guyer S41567. 4. *American Revolutionary Soldiers of Franklin County, Pennsylvania.* 5. Sons of the American Revolution Membership Application. 6. Daughters of the American Revolution Magazine Vol. 46, Pennsylvania's Patriotic Women during the Revolution.

Sir, There is a Little Matter of the Interest

The Battle of Trois-Rivieres (Three Rivers) was fought on June 8, 1776 with the purpose of removing the province of Quebec from British control. The Americans lost the battle, and during their retreat from Quebec American's wounded were treated by Ursuline nuns at their convent on Trois-Rivieres. All these years the nuns kept a record of the expenses related to treating the soldiers. The amount was $104 and on July 4, 2009 the American Consul-General repaid the debt to the nuns. The Ursulines estimated that in today's money, and with interest the bill would have amounted to $20 million dollars.

Source: 1. *Trois-Rivieres-A Tale of Tenacity by Monique Roy-Sole*, Canadian Geographic, May 23, 2009.

Independence Comes Down to Just One Vote

In June of 1776 the Continental Congress began the debate on the Resolution of Independence, which was should we, or should we not declare our independence from England. When the final vote was taken, it came down to one vote deciding it. The Pennsylvania delegation was split; two for independence and two against.

John Morton was a fifty-one year old farmer from Pennsylvania who had the deciding vote. All eyes in the great room were on him. He sat for a few minutes staring at the floor, and then he rose in his chair and quickly said, *"I vote yes."* With just three words a new nation was born.

He died the next year, becoming the first signer of the Declaration of Independence to die. His vote made him very unpopular with many people, and on his death bed he said, *"They will live to see this act to have been the most glorious service that I ever rendered my country."*

National Archives

Sources: 1. *Voices of the American Revolution: Stories of Men, Women, and Children Who Forged Our Nation* by Kendall F. Haven. 2. D.A.R. Lineage Book, Vol. 58, page 174.

Look What We Found

When Washington crossed the Delaware in retreat in 1776 with the British in pursuit he wanted all materials left behind destroyed. Joshua Mersereau and his son Joshua Jr. asked if they could go back across the river and search the shore. On the other side of the river they found two Durham boats, which were boats used to carry troops and were purposely sunk by the Tories for later use. They raised the boats and destroyed them preventing the British from using them. Had Joshua and his son not done this, the British could have crossed the Delaware and might have destroyed Washington's army.

Source: 1. D.A.R. Lineage Book, Vol. 143, page 289.

You Can't Leave Until You Have Tasted My Cake

After the Battle of Brooklyn in August of 1776, General Washington's troops began to retreat. In September of the same year British General William Howe landed troops in Kip's Bay in order to trap the retreating Americans.

Mary Murray, a patriot, realized the Americans were within a mile from her home on Long Island, and that the British had twice the number of soldiers. If the British were not stopped, the Americans would be trapped and captured. As the British troops approached Mary's home, she asked the officers if they would like to stop and have cake and wine.

The British officers agreed, and Mary fed them while her daughters entertained them. Mary had a maid go upstairs and keep watch from the window to let her know when the American troops were safely withdrawn. By the time the meal was completed, the Americans had withdrawn to safety.

Legend portrays Mary as tempting the British officers with her charms. However, it should be noted that Mary was in her fifties and was the mother of twelve children. A few historians doubt that the event even took place. The story of Mary was developed into two Broadway plays: *Dearest Enemy* in 1925, and *A Small War on Murray Hill* in 1957.

Sources: *Revolutionary Women: In the War for American Independence* edited by Lincoln Diamant. 2. *Seventeen Seventy-Six* by David McCullough.

Shouldn't You Be in School?

On September 1, 1776 Richard Knight joined Captain John Betty's Company in the 5th Pennsylvania Regiment under the command of Colonel Robert Magaw. Richard fought at the Battle of Brandywine on September 11, 1777. More troops fought at this battle than any other battle in the American Revolution. The battle was also the longest single-day battle during the war and with continuous fighting for eleven hours. Richard also fought at the Battles of Germantown and Monmouth, and in 1779 he took part in the Sullivan Expedition. He remained on the rolls until January 17, 1780. Richard served nearly four years and was in four major battles. He left the army a veteran at the age of thirteen.

Sources: 1. Sons of the American Revolution Application. 2. D.A.R.

I'm Just a Silly Little Boy

Before the Battle of White Plains in October of 1776, Ariel Bradley age eight was chosen by General George Washington to enter the British lines to learn their numbers and troop distributions. Ariel took an old horse and a bag of grain under the pretense of going to the mill. When he rode into the British camp, he was as expected arrested. Ariel showed no fear or any unusual curiosity as he was taken to British officers for questioning. During this time he was making mental notes of the information he was sent to retrieve.

The British officers questioned Ariel who acted unconcerned and innocent, and eventually the officers let him go. They thought him to be more of a fool than a spy. As Ariel was leaving one British officer was heard to say, *"I believe this little devil will betray us."* Ariel later returned to the camp of General Washington with the information he was sent to gather.

Sources: 1. D.A.R. Lineage Book, Vol. 143. 2. D.A.R. Plaque. 3. Sons of the American Revolution Application. 4. Ohio Historical Marker in Mogadore.

A Hard Man to Kill

Jonathan Nickerson joined the army at the age of fourteen in 1776. Years after his service he applied for a pension and told the following story,

"A little distance below and east of White Plain we were overtaken by a party of British horse 70 or 80 in number said to belong to Colonel Delanceys corps. The horse came upon the path full speed and were in the midst of the cattle and horses before the party could move through the drove calling out "Surrender you damned rebels surrender" Several of the party were struck down when I presented my musket to surrender instead of receiving it I was struck down to the ground my skull fractured and cut through the bone for four inches or more and while lying on the ground was rode over and struck four strokes in the head and several in the body with a cutlass. No one of the party escaped except the pilot (named Honam) to carry the news to camp one of the party after the British left was alive & was brought in by the inhabitants to the house where I was."

"After I had been stripped of my neckcloth and silver shoe buckles and my pockets searched by the British, they discovered that I was not dead for I had lain perfectly still before plunder. The captain then asked me to what troops I belonged and how many there were of the party which I told him. Capt said one had escaped and asked me if I could ride with them to the British lines. I answered I could not tell as I did not know how bad my wounds were. I was then put on the with them perhaps half or three quarters of a mile when I grew faint with the loss of blood and clung down by the horses mane in the road and told them I could go no further with them. Someone asked "shall we kill him?" The captain said "no let him alone he will die soon himself."

"I asked capt to tell the people in the next house to come and bring me in. Said he would & presumed he did for in about half an hour a number of the inhabitants living between the lines came and carried me into the house of one Joseph Hart in a blanket-they also brought one more of the party belonging to the same company by the name of O'Brien who died in about an hour. The next morning two doctors belonging as they said to the Continental line having been down to the British lines with a flag of truce called and cleaned and dressed my wounds."

"I remained at Hart's for fourteen days-during that time had not been dressed, undressed or out of the couch on which I was first laid. Late in the night of the fourteenth day a detachment

of British horse and foot commanded by the capt who made me prisoner came and put up to the house where I lay. He said it was more than he expected to find me alive and said something must be done or he would soon be off and fighting them again–Said he sound put me under parole and wrote two–each took one, the words of which I well remember. They were these "I Jonathan Nickerson, acknowledge myself a prisoner to the British army and do any thing prejudicial to the British army until exchanged and that I will come into the British lines as soon as able" signed by both–capt signed "Frederick Williams Capt Commdr, Frog's Neck" The same morning the British marched off towards the American lines."

About ten o'clock of the same day a party of militia commanded by capt Ichabod Doolittle of 25 or 30 men and a company of Continental troops commanded by Captain Fog belonging to New Hampshire it was said came to Harts house. I showed them my parole. They said they came purposely for me and I must go with them. They took and put me on a led horse and brought me to the American lines and from thence home to Ridgefield. I had not my own arms and accoutrements when taken and had to account for those taken. Soon after this I requested Ezra Nickerson to go to the lines and bring my equipments and clothing home and inquire of General Waterbury what I should do about answering my parole when able. Ezra told me that General Waterbury would see him and exchange soon and that I need not return for the remainder of my time."

Sources: 1. U.S. Pensioners 1818-1872. 2. Pension papers S28824.

Captain Molly

Margaret was a big woman, 5'8" tall and very strong. Her husband enlisted in the 1st Company of the Pennsylvania Artillery under the command of Captain Thomas Proctor, and Margaret went along with him. During the Battle of Fort Washington on November 16, 1776 British and Hessian troops stormed the fort. Margaret's husband was killed tending his cannon. His job was the position of matross, who was the person who loaded the cannon.

She stepped in and took his place during the battle which made herself a target. Grapeshot was fired at her and she was wounded in the shoulder, chest, and jaw. The British captured the fort, and Margaret was released with the other American wounded. She was taken to Philadelphia and never fully recovered from her wounds. She lost all use of her left arm.

In 1779 Pennsylvania awarded her $30 for her service, and in 1780 she received a small monthly pension, thus becoming the first woman to receive a pension from the United States government as a disabled soldier. She remained on the army muster list until the end of the war in 1783.

Before the end of the war she was assigned to an invalid regiment at West Point. At the Point she was called "Captain Molly", where she received a rum ration, smoked, cursed and hung out with the rest of the soldiers. She is buried at West Point.

Sources: 1. *Courageous Women: Thirty-Two Short Stories* by Connie Solano. 2. *Women Patriots of the American Revolution: a Biographical Dictionary* by Charles E. Claghorn. 3. Sketch of Margaret Corbin by Herbert Knotel is part of the West Point Museum collection. Photograph courtesy of West Point Museum Collection, United States Military Academy.

The First Commandos in the Revolution

In December of 1776 General Charles Lee, Washington's second in command, was captured by the British. The only way to get him back was a prisoner exchange but the Americans had no prisoner equal to the rank of General Lee. So Lt. Colonel William Barton came up with a plan to capture British General Richard Prescott in Newport, Rhode Island.

Barton selected forty of his best men, black and white, for the dangerous mission and asked for volunteers. Every man stepped forward. In the middle of the night they loaded into small boats, wrapped fabric around the oars to muffle the sound, and they rowed past British gunboats anchored in the harbor. They landed on the shore near the house where the General was staying. They quickly overpowered the guards and entered the house.

The door to the room where General Prescott slept was locked. Prince Jack Sisson, a large black man and former slave, charged the door using his own head as a battering ram, and on the second attempt the door broke. The Americans entered the room and took captive the General and his aid Major Barrington. The American and British Generals were later exchanged. Congress offered Barton a sword and promotion, ballads were written and sung, and all praised the 'sturdy negro' who broke through into the general's chamber grabbing him and hauling him out the door.

Within a year of Prescott's capture, Jack Sisson enlisted in the newly-formed First Rhode Island, made up mostly of freemen and slaves for whom freedom was granted upon joining. He fought well on his own turf in the Battle of Rhode Island and served out his time until war's end.

It should also be noted that General Prescott was the only officer of major rank who was captured and exchanged twice. The first time he was captured by Americans at Montreal and exchanged for American General Sullivan who was captured at the Battle of Long Island.

Sources: 1. *Black Heroes and Founders of the Great American Revolution*, posted by iusbvision on January 24, 2011. 2. *Captor of the Barefoot General* by Leonard Falkner, August 1960 American Heritage Magazine, 11:5. 3. *Colored Patriots of the American Revolution* by William C. Null, 1856.

But I'm Not Finished with My Letter

General Charles Lee was not fond of his commander General George Washington, because Lee thought he should have been appointed the commander of the American Army, and not Washington. Lee once said of Washington, *"He is not fit enough to command a Sergeant's Guard."*

Lee's army was supposed to join Washington's army in Pennsylvania. Probably due to his lack of respect for Washington, Lee set a very slow pace while marching toward his commander. Lee was captured by the British on December 13, 1776 at White's Tavern in Basking Ridge, New Jersey near his own camp. The night before Lee and a dozen of his guard stopped at the tavern for the night. He was only three miles away from his camp, but Lee was in no hurry.

That morning Lee was in his dressing gown writing letters when he was captured by a British patrol that had stopped at the tavern. They let the General throw a blanket over his dressing gown, tied him on a spare horse, and sent him to the British camp about eighty miles away. At least *"the man not fit enough to command a Sergeant's Guard"* was never captured by the British.

Sources: 1. *Washington: The Indispensable Man*, page 120. 2. *Dictionary of National Biography*, Charles Lee, 1892, pages 344-347.

Nothing to See Here, Get Some Rest

All schoolchildren are told about the surprise attack by George Washington's army on the Hessians soldiers on December 26, 1776 at Trenton. They are told that the Hessians were sleeping and were caught completely by surprise. But only a few people know why they were caught by surprise.

The Hessian Colonel Rall had received word from some local Tories that the Americans were planning a surprise attack. The Colonel ordered his men to be prepared and alert. Early in the day on December 25th, hours before Washington's men began marching to cross the Delaware, a small group of patriots from New Jersey raided one of the Hessian guard post. The patriots were not aware of Washington's plan to attack Trenton early the next morning.

The New Jersey patriots killed one Hessian and then fled back into the woods. Colonel Rall sent his men on patrols out into the woods to look for the rebels. They searched for hours and found no trace of any Americans soldiers. Colonel Rall called his men back in late that Christmas night thinking that there was no danger of attack. He ordered his men to get some rest and security around the camp was relaxed. The next morning Washington and his men stormed the camp and took the army by surprise, which was thanks to an unknown band of New Jersey patriots.

National Archives

Also, popular history likes to report that the Hessians were drunk from celebrating Christmas. Americans that fought in the battle say that the Germans were dazed and sleepy but no liquor had been consumed.

Sources: 1. *7 Leadership Lessons of the American Revolution* by John Antal. 2. *Bringing Back the Black Robed Regiment* by Dan Fisher.

A Little White Lie

Jeffrey Brace was born c. 1742 in Africa, and he was captured by slave traders at sixteen, shipped to Barbados, and sold. He was an enslaved sailor during the Seven Years War, which was fought between 1754 and 1763. After the war he was taken to Connecticut and sold again. In Connecticut he was sold three more times. Although literate he was blind in his later years, and he narrated the story of his life in the book *The Blind African Slave*.

He joined the 6th Connecticut Regiment under the command of Colonel Return Jonathan Megis. Jeffrey claims to have fought at the Battles of White Plains, Monmouth, Princeton, Newark, Froggs-point, and Horseneck. He wrote in his pension application about an incident that forced him to tell a small lie.

"We marched to West Point, and took winter quarters. While we remained here the soldiers played many boyish pranks. One Samuel Shaw, a brave soldier, but as complete a petty thief as ever graced a camp. He with myself and some others from our camp, the day before we were to be reviewed, by his Excellency, Gen, George Washington, concluded we would have a soldier like frolick."

"Accordingly we secretly stole from the lines, went to a Farm not many miles distant, which was occupied by a Tory. From him we stole a shoat [a sheep-goat hybrid]. *Shaw was the principle manager in this affair, and we got into camp just before day. We laid the Shoat in the middle of the camp, and in the language of gratitude, began conversing upon our success; but short was our confab."*

"As we soon saw the frothing Tory coming for his Hog. We immediately covered ourselves with our blankets and effected to be asleep. He recognized his property; he went to the Col. To whose regiment we then belonged; and reported that we had stolen one of his shoats. Col. Megs, came immediately to our company, and with a contenance, that plainly bespoken a determination of punishing us if guilty. He asked how we came by that Shoat; I answered immediately that the owner had brought it for sale, but that manner of conservation (knowing him to have been a tory) we unanimously suspected him to have come as a spy, and were determined to keep the Shoat until the officers might have an opportunity of being acquainted with his designs. My fellow soldiers were glad of the opportunity of confirming the truth of my assertion—which so completely satisfied the Col. Of our innocence, together with the circumstance of its lying in fair view, in the middle of the Camp—that he severely reprimanded the man for his insult on him and his soldiers. The man a little frighten at so unexpected a charge of guilt that he really had the appearance of a condemned culprit, and was glad to escape with his dead pig upon his back."

Sources: 1. *The Blind African Slave or Memories of Boyrereau Brinch, Nick-Named Jeffrey Brace* by Benjamin Prentiss, 1810. 2. Pension Application S41461.

They Will Never Be of Use in Battle

On September 6, 1776 the first submersible, an underwater vessel, was used by the Americans. It was launched at eleven o'clock at night to sink the British flagship HSM *Eagle*. The lone crew member of the *Turtle* was Sergeant Ezra Lee, a volunteer. He made two attempts to attach a bomb to the hull of the British ship and both failed. Because of fatigue and the effects of breathing too much carbon dioxide, Lee abandoned his mission. It was the first recorded use of a submarine to attack a ship. In 1785 Washington wrote to Thomas Jefferson, *"I then thought, and still think, that it was an effort of genius."*

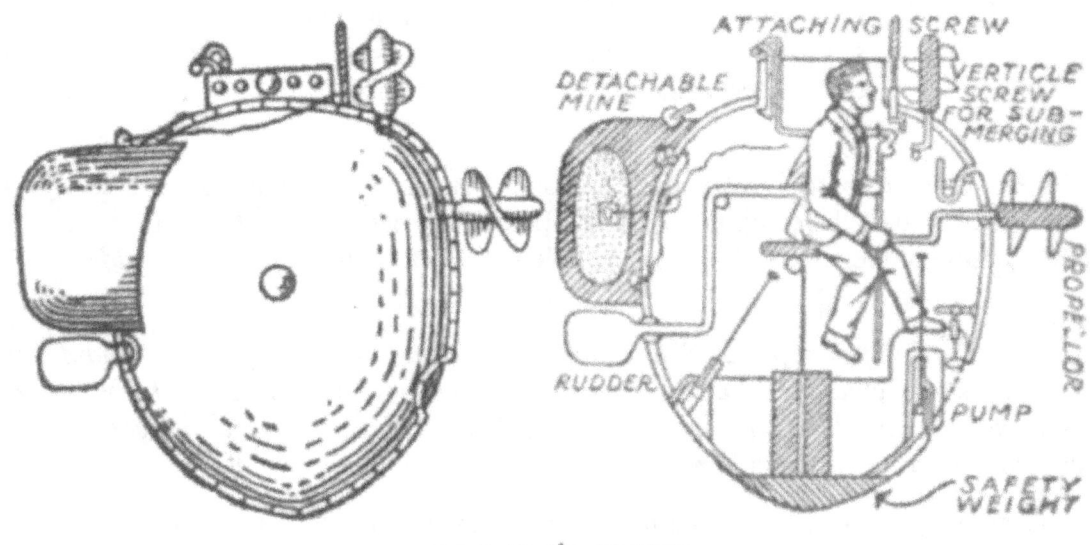

BUSHNELL'S TURTLE

A History of Sea Power by William Oliver Stevens, Allan Westcott, Allan Ferguson Westcott Published by G. H. Doran Company, 1920, pg. 294. {PD-1923}

Sources: 1. Diary of Andrew Hunter. 2. *Ships and Seamen of the American Revolution* by Jack Coggins. 3. *The Submarine Pioneers* by Richard Compton-Hall.

I Don't Remember Her Voting on Independence

Is there a woman's signature on the Declaration of Independence? If you look closely at a printed copy you will see the name of Mary Katharine Goddard.

The founding fathers first asked John Dunlap to print 200 copies of the document. The only names on this printed version were John Hancock and Secretary Charles Thomson, who is listed as a witness. There are twenty-five known copies of this document still in existence.

On January 18, 1777 the Second Continental Congress moved that the Declaration of Independence with all the signatories be printed and distributed. Mary Goddard offered her press for the task. Congress consented and her press became the second to print the document, and the first to contain typeset names of signatories. She printed at the bottom, *"Baltimore, in Maryland: Printed by Mary Katharine Goddard."* By printing her name at the bottom she knew she placed her life in danger.

Sources: 1. *Encyclopedia of the Age of Political Revolutions and New Ideologies, 1760-1815* edited by Gregory Fremont-Barnes, page 310. 2. *From Colonies to Country, 1735-1791* by Joy Hakim, pages 140-141.

If You Talk the Talk, You Must Be Prepared to Walk the Walk

The 6th Amendment of the U.S. Constitution states, *"In all criminal prosecutions, the accused shall enjoy the right to be confronted with the witness against him."* George Washington believed in this even before we had a constitution.

In 1777 American General Lincoln was surprised in his quarters at Bound Brook by the army of Lord Cornwallis. Lincoln barely had time to escape out a back door and run to safety. Hessian Colonel von Donop later wrote that General Lincoln *"must have retired profoundly undressed."*

General Lincoln soon discovered the reason the British got into his camp so easily was due to a farmer, who lived in the camp and gave the British the camp's countersign. Lincoln brought this to the attention of General Washington and demanded that the farmer, *"be made an example of."*

General Washington replied, *"Did you not tell me that the life of your informant depended on you secrecy, would you take up a Citizen & confine him without letting him know his crime or his accuser. No, let him alone for the present; watch him carefully, and if you can catch him in any other crime, so as to confront him by witness, we will then punish him severely."*

It became clear to General Lincoln that he had proposed to violate the very civil rights that he was fighting to establish.

Source: 1. *Journal or Historical Recollections of American Events during the Revolutionary War* by Elias Boudinot, 1894.

Mistaken Identity

Isaac Royal was born maybe in Maine on March 10, 1765, and died on November 20, 1816 in Piscataquis County, Maine. He married Tabitha Nason in 1786. He served as a cabin boy to John Paul Jones during the Revolutionary War. Isaac Royal joined the navy as a cabin boy to John Paul Jones (left) in the fall of 1777. He served on the *Ranger,* which sailed from Portsmouth on November 1, 1777. The *Ranger* had a crew of 140 men, sixteen guns, and was built at a cost of $65,000 Continental dollars. Its mission, the first of its kind in the war, was to go to the Irish Sea and begin raids on British warships.

The crew became a problem for Captain Jones, because they wanted to be privateers and not be sailors looking for a fight with warships. When the *Ranger* reached France, Jones and Ben Franklin obtained French funds to refit the ship to make it faster and more maneuverable. The ship's gun ports were disguised, so that the ship and crew could easily be mistaken for a British ship.

Isaac Royal told the following account to his son John, and it was passed down through the family, *"At one time when I was a cabin-boy with John Paul Jones, we were cruising in English waters and fell in with an English merchant ship, at night, and anchored near her. I think we were flying the English flag. In the early morning Capt. Jones invited the English captain on board for breakfast. The Englishman accepted the invitation and came to our ship with several of his officers. While at breakfast, Jones, unknown to the Englishmen, ordered the American flag to be run up to the masthead. Breakfast over the visitors were escorted on deck and Capt. Jones, directing their attention to the colors, said, 'Look at the handsome flag at the masthead, the colors under which I sail.' They did so, and to their intense chagrin and wrath saw the stars and stripes. They were made prisoners, and their vessel was taken as a prize."*

This occurred in Carrickergus Harbor in Ireland. The prize made the crew of the *Ranger* a little happier about sailing with Captain Jones. During this voyage Captain Jones destroyed and captured several British Ships.

Sources: 1. *John Paul Jones: Finding the Forgotten Patriot* by Robert L. Saunders. 2. *Collections of the Piscataquis County Historical Society, Issue 1* by Piscataquis County Historical Society, Dover, Maine. 3. Census 1810.

Maybe I Should Have Said Please

The Battle of Short Hills, also known as the Battle of Metuchen Meetinghouse, was fought on June 26, 1777. The fight was between the American General "Lord Stirling" and British Generals William Howe and Cornwallis. The Americans fought hard, but they were outnumbered and outgunned and were forced to retreat toward Westfield.

General William Howe — General Charles Cornwallis

While following the American retreat, Lord Cornwallis was near Westfield when he approached a farm house. The woman of the house, known in the area as "Aunt Betty" Frazee, was baking bread for the hungry American troops. Cornwallis approached her and said, *"I want the first loaf of bread that next comes out of that oven."* He then turned and sat under a large shade tree.

When the bread was done "Aunt Betty" took the bread to Cornwallis and told him, *"Sir, I give you this bread through fear, not in love."* Cornwallis was moved by her spirit and courage and told his men that none of them were to touch a single loaf of her bread.

Source: 1. *History of Union County, New Jersey, Vol. 1-2* by R.W. Ricord, 1897.

If I Comb My Hair Over It Doesn't Show

Many Native American historians say that scalping was not a New England tribal practice before contact with Europeans. It became a retaliatory act against the colonists. The colonies had offered scalp bounty as early as 1688. Massachusetts Bay Colony offered up to $60 for a Native American scalp. In Salem redeemed scalps hung along the walls of the town courthouse until 1785.

Scalping was a painful experience but did not always cause death. Nicholas Bovie was shot, tomahawked, and scalped by the Indians at Fort Stanwix in 1777. He recovered enough to return to duty and earned the nickname "Scalped Nick."

After the death of Nicholas his wife Polly filed for a widow's pension for his service. She described how Nicholas was injured,

"He was stationed at Fort Stanwix, and while on fatigue duty with a part about a mile from the Fort, the party being suddenly attacked by a party of Indians, who killed and wounded a number of the soldiers, he was wounded by two balls which passed through his right arm, by a tomahawk in the hip, which disabled him from running. When he was overtaken, scalped and left for dead. The soldiers from the Fort found him barely alive, he was carried to the Fort, where he lay about three months."

Several years after the war ended Nicholas had a relative who was involved in a scalping incident. Peter Bovie was at a fort in Deerfield, and he witnessed the scalping of a little girl by an Indian. Peter became angry by what he had seen, so he grabbed his rifle, left the fort, and tracked the Indian. When he overtook the Indian he fired and killed him. Peter then scalped the Indian and held it aloft. The young girl survived the scalping and lived to a ripe old age.

Sources: 1. *The Bloodied Mohawk: The American Revolution in the Words of Fort Planks Defenders and Other Mohawk Valley Partisans* by Kenneth D. Johnson. 2. Pension papers W16916. 3. *Captured by the Indians: 15 Firsthand Accounts, 1750-1870* by Frederick Drimmer. 4. *The Hoosac Valley* by Grace Greylock Niles, page 121. 5. *Hudson-Mohawk Genealogical and Family Memoirs Vol. III* by Cuyler Reynolds, pages 967-969.

Maybe We Need to Check a Little Closer

Robert Franklin was a soldier in Captain Smallwood's company of New York Militia. He was wounded at the Battle of Bennington and was falsely reported as having died in a hospital.

Source: 1. D.A.R. Lineage Book, Vol. 52, page 10.

Edward Byram served as a private in Captain Steven Bett's company of Connecticut Militia in 1777. In 1779 he and his daughter were taken prisoners by Indians and confined at Fort Niagara for nearly two years. He made it back home in October of 1781 and found himself mourned as dead.

Source: 1. D.A.R. Lineage Book, Vol. 54, page 215.

Sure I Trust You

During his stay at West Point General Washington frequently dined at the home of a nearby family. Suspicions had arisen about the honesty of his host, and some had accused the person of treachery to the American cause. One time the man was very insistent that Washington dine with him on a certain day and a certain hour. The host, aware of the suspicions that circled around him, suggested that Washington come alone without his usual guard. He said that this would prove that the General trusted him and the suspicions were unfounded. This insistence of a certain day and time aroused the suspicions of Washington, so he arrived at one o'clock which was an hour early for the dinner.

The host insisted that the two of them take a walk and enjoy a conversation. During the walk Washington noticed that the man seemed nervous and excitable. The General led the conversation to topics that might make the host betray his agitation. At one point Washington pointed out in the distance the British camp. He remarked to the man about the lack of principle that could induce men of American birth to trade the interests of their country and their patriotism for helping the British on the promise of a little gold.

The man became very agitated and nervous at the remarks and had no reply. At 1:45 the sound of British horsemen interrupted the men's conversation. Washington turned toward the noise and said, *"Bless me, sir. What cavalry are these approaching the house?"*

The host replied with a shaking voice, *"A party of British light horse who mean no harm, but are sent for my protection!"* Washington replied in a stern voice, *"British horse sent here while I am your guest! What does this mean sir?"*

As the horsemen arrived and dismounted, the host spoke with a little more courage in his voice, *"General, you are my prisoner." "I believe not,"* replied Washington in a calm voice. *"But sir, I know you are mine! Officer, arrest this traitor."*

The host was shocked to learn that Washington had ordered a company of Americans to disguise themselves as British cavalry and to arrive at the home at a designated time. Washington had suspected that his host was a false friend, and this ruse was designed to expose the man. The man later confessed that the British had offered him a large sum of money to betray General Washington. The British Calvary was to arrive at the house that day at 2 o'clock to capture the General.

At first Washington was going to make an example of the man, but the traitor's family begged for mercy. Washington pardoned the man.

Source: 1. *The Romance of the Revolution Being True Stories of Adventure, Romantic Incidences, Hairbreadth Escapes, and Heroic Exploits of the Days of '76* by Oliver Bell Bunce, pages 31-35.

Well Since You Put It That Way

In 1777 George Palmer Ransom, age fourteen, joined a company under the command of Captain Spalding. The company was present at the Siege of Fort Mifflin. During that battle British bullets were tearing through the fort, and men were falling on every side. A soldier in George's company threw himself on the ground and said, *"Nobody can stand this."* Captain Spalding looked at the man and calmly told him, *"Get up my good fellow, I should hate to have to run you through; you can stand it if I can."* The man got up and cheerfully returned to his duty.

Sources: 1. Pension Papers W2694. 2. *History of Westmoreland County, Pennsylvania, Vol. 1* by John Newton Boucher. 3. *A Genealogical Record of the Descendants of Captain Samuel Ransom of the Continental Army* by Captain Clinton B. Sears, 1882. 4. *New England Families, Genealogical and Memorial, Vol 2*, ed. by William Richard Cutter.

Hard Headed Irishman

Thomas Clarke, a sixty-five year old Irish immigrant, was a witness at the Battle of Brandywine and was taken prisoner by the British. The British told him to help fire a cannon during the battle. Thomas said he would not fire the cannon against his adoptive country so the British tied him to a cannon all day.

Source: 1. D.A.R. Lineage Book, Vol. 62, page 272.

Clinton Meet Clinton and then Meet Clinton

The Battle of Fort Clinton in October of 1777 is sometimes referred to as the Battle of the Clintons. George Clinton was the Governor of New York and he was also the General in command of Fort Montgomery. General George Clinton shared command of Fort Montgomery with his brother General James Clinton. General James Clinton was also in commanded of Fort Clinton a smaller fort less than a mile from Fort Montgomery. General Henry Clinton was the British General in command of the troops attacking Fort Montgomery.

Source: 1. *A Guide to the Battles of the American Revolution* by Theodore P. Savas, David J. Dameron.

If You Have Seen this Dog Please Call....

After the Battle of Germantown on October 4, 1777 a stray dog was found by some American troops. The dog was wearing an inscription on its collar indicating that he was the property of British General Howe which was the man that had just defeated them. General Washington had the dog returned to Howe with a polite note. This is an indication of how respectable gentlemen, even in war, were supposed to act.

Source: 1.*General Howe's Dog: George Washington, the Battle of Germantown, and the Dog who Crossed Enemy Lines* by Caroline Tiger.

Semper Fidelis

The first African American to fight in a Marine role was John Martin, also known as Keto. He was the slave of a Delaware man recruited in 1776, without his owner's permission. He served with the Marine platoon on the *Reprisal* for a year and a half and involved with hard ship-to-ship fighting. He was lost at sea with the rest of his unit when the brig sank in October 1777.

Source: 1. *Blacks in the Marine Corps* by Henry I. Shaw & Ralph W. Donnelly.

Sir, the Sign Clearly States Trunks Are Required

In the fall of 1777 a British fleet controlled Lake Champlain. The American army had to send important dispatches from one side of the lake to forces on the other side. There were no boats available so two Vermont men, Samuel Webster and Richard Wallace, volunteered to swim across the lake nearly three miles and deliver the dispatches. These dispatches were critical if the Americans were going to recapture Mount Independence on the Vermont side of the lake.

It was mid-October, and the water was very cold when the two men entered the water. They decided to swim naked, so the clothes would not slow them down in the water. They placed their clothes in a bundle and tied them to the back of their heads. During the swim they had to avoid British patrol boats that lurked in the lake. When they reached their destination, Samuel was so badly chilled that he could not get out of the water without the help of Richard. Their nighttime swim resulted in the recapture of Mount Independence.

Richard never recovered his health from the swim. Years later night fishermen in the area claimed they saw the ghost of a naked swimmer and heard teeth chattering.

Sources: 1. *Haunted Vermont: Ghosts and Strange Phenomena of the Green Mountain State* by Charles A. Stansfield, Jr. 2. D.A.R. Lineage Book, Vol 43, page 170.

Fact or Fiction: A Shot Taken and a Shot Not Taken Might Have Changed the Outcome of the Revolution

Both of the following accounts have historians divided on if they actually happened or not. Both could have altered the final outcome of the American Revolution.

A Shot taken: Timothy Murphy, 1751-1818, joined Daniel Morgan's newly formed Morgan's Riflemen. This group of 500 Americans were considered expert marksmen. To gain this recognition they were supposed to be able to hit a seven inch target at 250 yards.

During the Battle of Bemis Heights (the second Battle of Saratoga on October 7, 1777) American General Benedict Arnold noted that British General Simon Fraser was having success leading his troops against the Americans. Arnold told Colonel Daniel Morgan, *"that officer upon a grey horse* (Fraser) *is of himself a host, and must be disposed of."*

Morgan selected several of his men to shoot at General Fraser. Timothy Murphy climbed a tree and took aim at the target 300 yards away. His first shot hit the dirt in front of General Fraser, and the second shot grazed the General's horse. One of the British officers next to Fraser saw the bullet graze the General's horse and said to him, *"Sir, it is evident that you are marked out for particular aim; would it not be prudent for you to retire from this place?"*

The General replied, *"My duty forbids me to fly from danger."* At that moment the General was shot through his body and fell from his horse. He was taken from the battlefield and died the next morning.

Who fired the fatal shot? Many believed that Timothy Murphy shot the General with his third shot. General Fraser himself said he saw the man who shot him, and that the man was up a tree. Other people present at the battle said the General was killed by an old man with a long hunting gun and not by one of Morgan's men.

General Frazer was the idol of the British army, and the one officer above of all others, on whom General Burgoyne placed the greatest reliance. On his death-bed Fraser suggested to Burgoyne that he surrender in order to end the bloodshed. Burgoyne surrendered his army, and the battle became the turning point of the American Revolution. The British defeat encouraged the French to enter the war on the side of the Americans. The French provided men, money, and supplies to the Americans in their fight against the British. Had Fraser not been shot he could have very well have led the British to victory, and thus discouraging the French to aid the Americans.

The shot not taken: Captain Patrick Ferguson (1744-1780) was considered to be the finest shot in the British army. He and a few of his marksmen came upon a small group of American officers during the Battle of Brandywine on September 11, 1777. Ferguson and his men were hidden about 100 yards from the American officers.

One of the officers wore a dark green and blue uniform with a high cocked hat, the badge of the Commander-in-Chief. The Americans were in the sights of the British marksmen, when Ferguson gave the order not to fire but to advance on the unsuspecting men. Ferguson had decided to take the Americans prisoners.

The British approached the officers and ordered the Americans to dismount. Ferguson yelled, *"You are marked by rifles. Come in as my prisoners."* The Americans turned their horses and began to ride away. Ferguson aimed his rifle at the back of the fleeing man with the high cocked hat. Ferguson lowered his rifle and allowed the men to escape. He later said he did not want to shoot the officer in the back.

Some historians doubt that the officer was General Washington, because no commanding officer would have been riding near the enemy with armed soldiers as escorts. It was later confirmed that Washington was out doing recon in the area. Some believe that the man in the rifle sights of Ferguson was the Polish hero Count Casimir Pulaski.

If the man fleeing was General Washington, and if Ferguson had taken the shot and killed him, the American army may have lost the will to fight.

Sources: 1. *Untamed Leadership: A Journey Through the Instincts that Shape Us* by Brent A. Carter, pages 126-127. 2. Boy's Life, Feb. 1956 Vol. 46, No. 2, page 75. 3. *The Campaign of Lieut. Gen. John Burgoyne* by William L. Stone, 1877, pages 324-326. 4. Graham's American Monthly Magazine of Literature and Art, George Graham, Editor, Vol. XXX, 1847, page 212. 5. *History of Schoharie County, and Border Wars of New York* by Jeptha R. Simms, 1845, pages 259-260.

It's No Big Deal, It Happens All the Time

At the Battle of Red Bank on October 22, 1777 over 600 Americans repelled 900 Hessian troops who were trying to take Fort Mercer. During the battle Mrs. Whitall was in a room in her home inside the fort. She was on the second floor spinning on her wheel trying to pass time during the battle. A British cannon ball entered the attic just above her. The cannon ball rolled across the floor, down the stairs, and landed at the foot of the stairs no more than ten feet from where she was sitting. She got up and took her spinning wheel to the basement and continued her spinning.

Sources: 1. D.A.R. Lineage Book, Vol. 34. 2. *Forty Minutes by the Delaware "The Battle of Fort Mercer"* by Lee Patrick Anderson.

We Will Sleep Through Your Meeting

When the British occupied Philadelphia in 1777, they stationed soldiers in the homes of citizens. One of the homes belonged to the Darragh family. Lydia Darragh and her husband William were Quakers and therefore pacifists. However, their oldest son Charles fought in the Revolutionary War.

British General William Howe had moved into the house across the street from Lydia. She began providing her son Charles with information about the British troops by listening to talk around town and in her home. On the night of December 2, 1777 Lydia's home became the meeting place between General Howe and his staff. They were meeting to finalize the plans for an attack on Whitemarsh on the 4th of December, where General George Washington and his army was encamped.

Lydia told the British officers that she had sent her two youngest children to live in another city with relatives and that she and William had no other place to stay and would like to stay in their own home. The officers knowing that Lydia and her husband were Quakers, and thus they did not support the war, believed it would be safe to let them stay in the house.

The officers told Lydia they would meet in the parlor and Lydia and William should go upstairs and go to bed. They told Lidia they would awaken them when they had finish their meeting. Lydia pretended to go to sleep, but instead she listened to the officers through the door. She overheard them say they were going to make a surprise attack on Washington and would leave the city on December 4th. She jotted down notes on what she heard; Howe leaving on 4th with 5,000 men for Whitemarsh, thirteen pieces of cannon, baggage wagons, and eleven boats on wagon wheels.

Lydia quietly sneaked back to bed and pretended to be asleep when Major John Andre knocked several times at her door. Lydia got up and pretended to be sleepy and followed the officers to the front door of her house. She then extinguished the candles in the room and went to bed. She decided not to tell her husband of what she had heard.

Early that morning she told William she had to buy flour at Pearson's Mill. She was given permission by General Howe to cross British lines to go to Frankford to get her flour. Lydia walked three miles to Rising Sun, where she met Elias Boudinot, who was director of intelligence in Washington's army. Elias gave an account of his meeting in his journal,

"I was reconoitering along the Lines near the City of Philadelphia. — I dined at a small Post at the rising Sun about three miles from the City. — After Dinner a little poor looking insignificant Old Woman came in & solicited leave to go into the Country to buy some flour — While we were asking some Questions, she walked up to me and put into my hands a dirty old needle book, with various small pockets in it. surprised at this, I told her to return, she should have an answer — On Opening the needlebook, I could not find any thing till I got to the last Pocket, Where I found a piece of Paper rolled up into the form of a Pipe Shank. — on unrolling it I found information that General Howe was coming out the next morning with 5000 Men — 13 pieces of Cannon — Baggage Waggons, and 11 Boats on Waggon Wheels. On comparing this with other information I found it true, and immediately rode Post to head Quarters."

After her meeting with Boudinot, Lydia continued to Whitemarsh where she met Lt. Colonel Thomas Craig whom she knew. She also gave him the warning message, and then she made her way to the mill to pick up her flour and walk back home. The British later found the Americans waiting for them and their surprise attack was foiled and Washington's army was saved.

The British knew that someone must have alerted the Americans ahead of time. One officer questioned Lydia and asked if anyone was awake that night of their meeting in her home. Lydia said just she and her husband were present and they were asleep. The officer, satisfied with the answer, asked no further questions. Later Major Andre would report, *"One thing is certain, the enemy had notice of our coming, were prepared for us, and we marched back like a parcel of fools. The walls must have ears."*

Sources: 1. *Journal or Historical Recollections of American Events during the Revolutionary War* by Elias Boudinot, from His Own Original Manuscript, 1894. 2. *All the Daring of the Soldier* by Elizabeth Leonard. 3. *Glory, Passion, and Principle: the Story of Eight Remarkable Women at the Core of the American Revolution* by Melissa Lukeman Bohrer.

That's a New Way to Get a Husband

People fall in love in the strangest places. In 1777 Captain John Morrell was in Colonel William Bradford's Regiment during the Revolution. One day he was carrying dispatches from headquarters and needed to cross the Delaware River in a storm. The ferryman, because of the danger, refused to carry him across. A local girl Sally Wallace agreed to ferry him across, and the Captain was so impressed with her courage and patriotism that he married her that spring.

Source: 1. D.A.R. Lineage Book, Vol. 53, page 363.

Chapter 4

"You say to your soldier, 'Do this' and he does it. But I am obliged to say to the American, 'This is why you ought to do this' and then he does it." "With regard to military discipline, I may safely say that no such thing existed in the Continental Army." Baron Von Steuben

The Winds of War Begin to Change - 1778

Great changes began to take place with the American army in the winter of 1778. During the encampment at Valley Forge the army was reorganized into five divisions. Baron Von Steuben had been given the task of teaching the troops the essentials of military drills, tactics, and discipline. To combat the shortage of enlistments, General Washington had reversed his earlier decision about enlisting blacks and gave recruiting officers permission to enlist them. In January of 1778 the General gave his approval to Rhode Island to raise an entire regiment of black slaves. This led to the formation of the 1st Rhode Island Regiment.

On February 6, 1778 one of the most important events of the war occurred. France signed the Treaty of Alliance with the United States, and it signaled their formal recognition of the United States. This means that France would send men, supplies, and ships to aid the American cause. When the news reached Valley Forge each man was given an extra gill of rum to celebrate. Washington celebrated with his officers, including the popular French officer General Lafayette.

In June Washington fought the British army to a standstill at the Battle of Monmouth. The training the Americans received at Valley Forge under Von Steuben proved that they could stand toe-to-toe with a superior number of British troops and fight them to a draw. After a full day of fighting, the longest battle of the Revolution, the British broke off the attack and marched to New York City.

The Battle of Monmouth was the last major battle fought in the north. During 1778 a little over a dozen battles were fought between the Americans and British troops. Neither side could obtain an advantage over the other, so a stalemate began. The British statesman William Pitt spoke out in Parliament calling for peace with America and for them to unite with Britain against their enemy France. Many members of Parliament, who were once sympathetic with the American cause, were now against them. They were angry that the Americans had joined with Britain's long time enemy. The British knew that a new strategy was needed in the colonies if they were going to defeat the rebels.

During this stalemate General Washington began to turn his attention to dealing with the threats from the Tories and their Indian allies. He organized several expeditions to attack Indian villages in order to kill or capture all inhabitants.

But Can He Do It In a Robe?

John Marshall was the fourth Chief Justice of the Supreme Court of the United States from 1801 to 1835. He was the longest serving Chief Justice and probably the most famous and influential in the history of the United States. In his early 20's he was a Captain in the 4th Virginia regiment at Valley Forge.

He was an athletic young man and enjoyed running and jumping. While at Valley Forge he was nicknamed "Silver Heels" for the white yarn in the heels his mother had sewn into his stockings. He would run races in his stocking against other soldiers and rarely lost. He could also vault over a pole "laid on the heads of two men as high as himself." John Marshall was six feet tall.

Sources: 1. *The Life of John Marshall* by Albert Jeremiah Beveridge, page 132. 2. *John Marshall: Definer of a Nation* by Jean Edward Smith, page 64.

He Could Make You Blush in Three Languages

Every school child learned how Baron Von Steuben trained the American soldiers at Valley Forge and turned them into a disciplined fighting force. Some may have learned that he was not an actual Baron, and was no longer in the Prussian army, when he offered his services to the cause of the patriots without pay or rank.

What most people do not know is that he spoke very little English, so Washington appointed a German speaking officer, Captain John Walker, as a translator. In addition, since the Baron spoke French, Washington also appointed Colonel Alexander Hamilton and General Nathanael Greene to translate the drill instructions to the troops from French to English.

The Baron wanted to demonstrate his new style of drill that the Americans would use. So, a company of soldiers from the Pennsylvania Line were there to follow his orders through the translator. The Baron told Captain Walker that he must translate in English every word he said, as he spoke. The Captain tried to tell the Baron why he shouldn't. *"You will translate in English exactly what I say,"* the Baron harshly demanded in German.

Not wishing to disobey the Baron, Walker repeated every order from the Baron in English. Again the Baron gave an order in German, and again it was translated in English. The Baron looked puzzled as to why the men were not responding to the commands. An aid to General Washington explained to the General that the men selected were all Pennsylvania Dutch, and they spoke only German.

As word about the mistake spread through the ranks, the men along with General Washington began to laugh. When the mistake was translated to the Baron, a broad smile began to spread across his face which was followed by a deep belly laugh.

At times the Baron would get angry at the way the soldiers trained, so he would cuss them out in German or French and then have the translators repeat the angry words to the men in English.

The men had never been cussed out in three languages. However, his salty language made the men feel that the Baron was one of them.

Sources: 1. *The Life of Frederick William Von Steuben* by Frederick Kapp, 1859, pages 94-140. 2. *Frederick William Von Steuben and the American Revolution* by Joseph B. Doyle, 1913 pages 73-100.

The Great Snowball Fight Part II

In 1778 there was another snowball fight, this time between Virginia and Pennsylvania troops. General Washington then issued a General Order forbidding on pain of severe punishment any person belonging to the army throwing snowballs at each other.

Source: 1. Pension Application of Isaac Artis S39943.

The Battle of the Kegs

The British fleet was in the harbor of Philadelphia on January 6, 1778, and American Colonel Borden enlisted an inventor by the name of David Bushnell to devise a way of sinking the ships. Bushnell gathered a large number of kegs, filled them with gun powder, and fixed them to explode upon contact while floating in the harbor. He released them to float down the Delaware River to float toward the British ships.

The British ships were positioned in the harbor to avoid floating ice, and as a result only one keg came in contact with a ship. It exploded causing little damage other than killing two curious young boys. The explosion alerted the British and their soldiers raced to the wharves and were ordered to shoot at any piece of wood in the water.

Francis Hopkinson wrote a song, which sarcastically praises the "courage" of the British troops. It was a defiant song to show that the Americans did not propose to give up. Here are a couple of verses of the song, "The Battle of the Kegs":

"These kegs now hold the rebels bold,

Pack'd up like pickled herring;

And they're come down t' attack the town

In this new way of ferrying.

The soldier flew; the sailor too;

And scar'd almost to death, Sir,

Wore out their shoes to spread the news,

And ran till out of breath, Sir."

Sources: 1. *A Military Journal During the American Revolutionary War: From 1775 to 1783* by James Thacher, 1823. 2. *Songs and Ballads of the American Revolution* by Frank Moore, 1856.

Third Time Was Not a Charm

After spending a cold winter at Valley Forge, Captain Charles Cameron was sent to Augusta County, Virginia to recruit troops for the American Army. On his way back to his Company, Charles and his men captured a Tory on the bank of the Potomac River. They decided to convert their prisoner by baptism into a loyal Patriot. They took him down to the river and threw him in the water.

The prisoner came up for air and shouted, *"Hurrah for King George!"* The Americans again dunked him in the water. The Tory again surfaced and shouted, *"Long live King George!"* Once again the man was pushed underwater for a longer period of time. He rose for the third time and shouted, *"King George forever!"*

The men looked at Captain Cameron with a puzzled look on their faces. The Captain ordered his men, *"Loose him and let him go, he is unconvertible."*

Source: 1. *Revolutionary Reader, Reminiscences and Indian Legends* by Sophie Lee Foster, page, 139.

I Just Happen to be Floating By

Nicholas Johnston was born on February 24, 1764 in Dumfries, Scotland, and about the age of thirteen he was conscripted into the British Army. In 1778 he deserted and floated down the Hudson River in the winter to join the American Army.

Sources: 1. Tombstone 2. The Official Roster of the Soldiers of the American Revolution Buried in the State of Ohio.

In Other Words, No!

Rev. Robert Smith enlisted as a private to successfully defend a fort from the British in June of 1778. One writer later wrote, *"The late Bishop Smith shouldered his musket, and amidst scenes of the greatest danger, both by precept and by example stimulated to intrepid resistance."*

In 1780 Charleston was captured by the British, and Pastor Smith was taken prisoner and his property confiscated. He was watched closely, and was soon offered his freedom, his pulpit, and property, if he would take an oath of loyalty to the crown. He refused saying, *"Rather would I be hanged by the King of England than go off and hang myself in shame and despair like Judas."* In June of 1781 he and other prisoners were transferred to Philadelphia, and in 1782 Smith was released. In 1795 he was elected the first Bishop of the Diocese of South Carolina.

Sources: 1. *Anecdotes of the Revolutionary War* by Alexander Garden, page 199. 2. *The American Revolution and Righteous Community* by Robert Smith, pages 22-26. 3. *From Its European Antecedents to 1791—The United States Army Chaplaincy* by Parker C. Thompson, 1978, page 171. 4. *Dictionary of American Biography*, 1936, 9:336.

The American Gunga Din

Most school children are told the story of "Molly Pitcher" who during the Battle of Monmouth brought water to the soldiers on the battlefield. Then they tell how her husband was either wounded or dropped from heat exhaustion while firing his cannon. Molly then took his place at the cannon during the battle. That is where the story usually ends, yet there is more to the story.

During the battle a British musket ball passed between her legs and tore off the bottom of her petticoat. She made a quick remark to the effect of, *"Well if that had been higher it could have been worse."* When the battle had ended, General Washington wanted to know who the woman was that he had seen loading the cannon. He issued a warrant making her a noncommissioned officer. Years later she liked using the nickname *"Sergeant Molly."*

In her later years she was often seen in the streets of her town wearing a striped skirt, wool stockings, and a ruffled cap. The people in town liked her even though they said she *"often cursed like a soldier."* In 1822 Pennsylvania awarded her an annual pension of $40 for her service. It is believed that Molly Pitcher got her last name, when during the battle soldiers that needed water would cry out, *"Molly—pitcher!"*

> *"Moll Pitcher she stood by her gun,*
> *And rammed the charges home, sir,*
> *And thus on Monmouth's bloody field,*
> *A sergeant did become sir."*

Sources: 1. *They Called Her Molly Pitcher* by Anne Rockwell. 2. A *Short History of Molly Pitcher, the Heroine of the Battle of Monmouth* by John B. Landis.

Forget the Handshake, Let's Just Smoke a Peace Pipe

Moses Nelson wrote about an encounter with Shawnee Indians on June 24, 1778: *"In the month of August ensuing when ten Frenchmen and Captain Blackfish the Shawnee's Chief with 340 warriors appeared in sight of the Fort, and professed friendship upon condition that Colonel [Daniel] Boone would surrender the fort into their possession, Colonel Boone and his men declined to accede to this proposition, and Captain Blackfish proposed a treaty, which was agreed to – the next day Colonel Boone and his officers were met by Blackfish and his Chiefs at a Spring about 60 yards from the Fort. Accordingly they proceeded to the appointed place, at the conclusion of said treaty, Blackfish said the custom among them was for two Indians to take hold of one white man, and shake hands strong to make a lasting treaty, when the Indians had got hold of the white men's hands they attempted to take prisoners of them, the men from the Fort fired on the Indians, they ran and all our men got into the Fort safe and unhurt, except one man who received a slight wound. The Indians then attacked the Fort and besieged the Fort for 9 days & nights without a cessation of hostilities, they then raised the siege, the Indians continued very troublesome throughout the whole Country."*

Source: Pension application of Moses Nelson R7585.

Modern Cain and Able

On July 3, 1778 a bloody battle took place between Tories and Patriots in Wyoming, Pennsylvania. Some of the Tories supported by the British and the Patriots were friends and neighbors before the war. As a result, their emotions and hatred ran deep and anytime they fought each other it was a vicious battle.

A force of nearly 600 Tories and Indians, led by Colonel John Butler, invaded Wyoming Valley and were met by nearly 360 patriot militiamen. Only a handful of the patriots survived the battle and about 260 scalps were taken by Indians.

The patriot leader was Colonel Butler, no relation to his counterpart, and he related the following event. He had escaped the battle with another soldier, Giles Slocum. Just below the battlefield on a small island in the Susquehanna River Giles was hiding in some bushes. There he was witness to the meeting of the Pensell brothers, John and Henry.

John was a Tory and Henry was a Patriot. Henry had lost his gun, and upon seeing his brother John, fell to his knees and begged for his life to be spared. John looked at his brother and called him a damned rebel, and he began to load his weapon while Henry continued to beg for his life. Henry told John that if he would spare him, he would serve him for the rest of his life.

John finished loading his gun and Henry said to him, *"You won't kill your brother will you?"* John replied, *"Yes I will as soon as look at you, you are a damned rebel."*

John then shot him and afterwards went up and struck him four or five times with a tomahawk and scalped him. Giles Slocum made his escape that evening.

Sources: 1. *Sacred Scripture, Sacred War* by James P. Byrd. 2. *Journals of the Military Expedition of Major General John Sullivan* by Frederick Cook, Section about Rev. William Rogers, 1887.

Treason Seems to Run In the Family

Rev. Alexander McWhorter met George Washington, who was in Newark on his way north to take command of the Continental Army in Massachusetts. In 1776 the pastor joined the army and became a personal chaplain of George Washington. He crossed the Delaware and fought with Washington at Trenton on December 26, 1776.

George Washington wrote to him on October 12, 1778 and requested his assistance. Washington wrote, *"There are now under sentence of death, in the provost, a Farnsworth and Blair, convicted of being spies from the enemy, and of publishing Continental currency. It is hardly to be doubted but that these unfortunate men are acquainted with many facts respecting the enemies affairs, and their intentions which we have not been able to bring them to acknowledge. Besides the humanity of affording them the benefit of your profession, it may in the conduct of a man of sense answer another valuable purpose—And Whole it serves to prepare them for the other world, it will naturally lead to the intelligence we want in your inquiries into the condition of their spiritual concerns. You will therefore be pleased to take the charge of this matter upon yourself, and when you have collected in the course of your attendance such information as they can give you will transmit the whole to me. I am Sir &c"*. [signed] *G W*

John Blair and David Farnsworth were convicted for spying and possessing a large sum of counterfeit money and were sentenced to death. The use of counterfeit money was a form of strategy used in warfare for centuries. The purpose was to flood the enemy's economy with the fake money, which would drive down the worth of the real money resulting in economic collapse. The two men were captured with over $10,000 of fake currency. Washington declined to spare either man and they were executed on Rocky Hill at Hartford on November 3, 1778. A distant relative of David's, John Farnsworth, was convicted of spying for Japan during the 1930's. John, a naval officer, served eleven years in prison.

Sources: 1. Founders online National Archives. 2. *From Its European Antecedents to 1791—The United States Army Chaplaincy* by Parker C. Thompson, 1978, page 147. 3. *The Chaplains and Clergy at the Battle of Monmouth* by Chaplain Stanley Cuyler, 1986, pages 13 and 17. 4. *The Chaplains and Clergy of the Revolution* by Joel Tyler Headley, 1864, pages 327-30. 5. *Appleton's Cyclopedia of American Biography,* Vol 8, page 269. 6. D.A.R. Lineage Book, Vol. 2, page 131.

Chapter 5

"General Arnold is gone to the Enemy." Letter from George Washington to Nathaniel Wade, Sept. 25, 1780.

The War Shifts to the South 1779-1780

Up until this time most of the fighting has been in the north. Since the war was at a stalemate there, British strategy was to take the fight to the south. Southern ports could be captured, which would hamper the influx supplies needed by the Americans. There were more Tories in the south who would fight for the British. Also, large groups of recent immigrants lived there and would still be friendly to England.

The south contained a large number of slaves that could be captured and encouraged to join with the British. Slave owners, especially in the south, were concerned that training and arming black men could lead to a black uprising. A group of Carolina slave owners stated, *"There must be great caution used* [allowing blacks into the military] *lest our slaves when armed might become our master."*

As the war shifted to the south, more southern black men were allowed to join. Georgia and South Carolina remained opposed to having blacks serve in the military. Some historians believe that if South Carolina and Georgia had allowed their slaves to fight, it could have shortened the length of the war.

Late in 1778 the British captured the port city of Savannah and controlled the coastline of Georgia. In 1780 they captured Charleston, and their victory at the Battle of Camden gave them control of much of South Carolina. The British victory at Charleston was the worst defeat of the Americans in the Revolution. General Lincoln surrendered his army of over 3,000 to the British. Many of the American prisoners would later die in British prison ships.

British confidence now was so high that General Clinton divided his army and sailed to New York City. He left behind General Cornwallis and his army of over 8,000 men to take control of the south. Victory over the rebels seemed a real possibility now.

Help from the Tories was limited in North Carolina and Virginia, and fighting the Americans in these areas became a guerrilla war. Many American victories were achieved this way in 1780 due to the leadership of Francis Marion and Nathanael Greene. The American army now played a cat-and-mouse game with the larger British army of Cornwallis.

During these two years the Americans lost most of their battles with the British. They did, however, achieve a major victory at the Battle of Kings Mountain on October 7, 1780. The victory helped to keep North Carolina out of British control, and it was a tremendous morale booster for the patriots. Over 1,000 of the enemy were killed, wounded, or captured.

Now That's Using Your Head

On February 14, 1779 Stephen Heard was one of the Americans captured by the hated Tories. The captured men were taken to Fort Cornwallis in Augusta, Georgia and imprisoned. When Heard's slave Mammy Kate learned that her master was in prison, she mounted his horse Lightfoot, took another horse, and rode about fifty miles to the prison.

She left the horse in a safe place outside of town and devised a plan to free Stephen. She got a clothes basket and went to the fort offering to do washing for the British officers. She soon gained the trust of the officers due to her good work. She asked if she could wash Heard's clothes. At first the officers declined saying that he was going to hang soon. She replied, *"Let him hang in clean clothes."*

They finally agreed, so Kate would visit Heard twice a week. She would take and return his clothing in a basket that she carried on top of her head. She also would sneak cake into Heard's cell by putting it between her breasts. She later told her children, *"I had to put dat bread in my bosom to get it to master. But I always took it out 'fore I got dar, 'cause he was might perticler."*

One evening as the sun was going down, she left Heard's cell with his clothes in the basket on top of her head. As she passed by the guards, it would be the last time they would ever see her. In the basket, covered by some clothes was Heard. Luckily, Heard was a small man and Kate was described *"as the biggest and tallest black woman"* local people had ever seen.

As soon as she was out of sight of the guards, she let Heard out and the two ran to where the horses were hidden. On the ride back a grateful Heard told her he was going to set her free for saving his life. She told him he could set her free, but she would never set him free. She was comfortable living on the plantation owned by Heard. Heard, who later became governor of Georgia, did set her free, gave her a small tract of land, and a four-roomed home that she lived in until her death.

Sources: 1. *Grandmother Stories from the Land of Used-to-Be: Atlanta, Georgia* by Howard Meriwether Lovett. 2. *History of Elbert County, Georgia 1790-1935* by John H. McIntosh. 3. Kate Book. Com, a Website for Kates, by Kates, and About Kates.

Never Kill a Prized Turkey

Nancy Hart or Aunt Nancy, as many called her was a rough frontier woman. She was described as about six feet tall with red hair and a smallpox scarred face. She was also cross-eyed and she was not exactly a thing of beauty. What she lacked in beauty, she made up in courage and spirit.

One day in 1779 five or six British soldiers and Tories came to her house and demanded information about the location of a certain patriot leader. A short time earlier the patriot had been at her cabin, and Nancy had helped him escape. She told the Tories that no one had been in her cabin for days. The men believed that she was lying, they grew angry, and one of the men shot her prized turkey. He handed the dead bird to Nancy and demanded that she cook it for them. Nancy sent her thirteen year old daughter, Sukey, supposedly out to the spring for water, but told the girl to blow a prearranged signal on a horn to alert the neighbors.

Meanwhile, the men had stacked their rifles in a corner of the cabin and were drinking wine and corn liquor and relaxing by the fire. Since the men were ignoring her, she began to pass their rifles out through a hole in the cabin wall to her daughter outside. One of the men saw her and began to approach her, so she pointed a rifle toward him and ordered him to stop.

Either the man did not think she would shoot or, as some people told the story, since she was cross-eyed, the man wasn't sure if she was looking at him or not. Regardless of the reason he advanced toward her, and she shot him dead. Another man made a move toward her, and she grabbed another rifle and shot and wounded him. Nancy grabbed another rifle, and blocking the doorway she ordered the men to surrender. One of the men said, *"Yes we will surrender, let's shake hands on the strength of it."* Now Nancy was guilty of not being attractive, but not guilty of being stupid. She pointed the rifle at the men and told them to sit down. She held off the remaining men until her husband and neighbors arrived to help.

Her husband wanted to shoot the men, but Nancy, who was probably still angry about her turkey, insisted that the men hang. The remaining British were taken out to a tree and hung. Years later many people believed this story to just be an old folk tale. Nancy and her husband had moved off and the cabin was falling apart. In 1912 workmen were digging near the site of the old cabin and unearthed a row of six skeletons, some in tattered British uniforms, laying side by side.

Nancy Hart from *Stories of Georgia* by Joel Chandler Harris. American Book Company, 1896.

Sources: 1. *Nancy Hart, Georgia Heroine of the Revolution: The Story of the Growth of a Tradition* by E. Merton Coulter, Georgia Historical Quarterly 39, June 1955. 2. *Nancy Hart: Too Good Not to Tell Again in Georgia Women: Their Lives and Times* by John Thomas Scott, Vol. 1. 3. *Women Patriots of the American Revolution a Biographical Dictionary* by Charles E. Claghorn.

A Thirty Year Grudge

At the Battle of Brier Creek on March 3, 1779 the American militia under the command of General Ashe was caught by surprise by the British and their Tory allies. The Americans ran from the camp leaving their cook fires burning and many of the men threw down their weapons without firing a shot.

American General Thomas Eaton fled from his tent in such a hurry that he did not have time to put his boots on. Eaton had a small foot and wore a boot of unusual finish and neatness. The Tory leader Colonel Hamilton knew Eaton and recognized the boots as his. He purchased them from the soldier that had taken them from the tent.

After the war Colonel Hamilton and General Eaton were at a dinner party given by Willie Jones in 1809. Hamilton returned Eaton's riding boots that he had taken from Eaton's tent during the battle. Eaton, it was reported, became enraged and threw the boots across the table at Hamilton's head.

Source: 1. *North Carolina 1780-81 Being a History of the Invasion of the Carolinas by the British Army under Lord Cornwallis* by David Schenck, 1889, pages 306-7.

I Can't See Where I'm Going, but I Can See Where I've Been

In 1779 George Duncan was a member of a Virginia regiment camped near Richmond, Virginia. A resident near there by the name of James Blain came into the camp to purchase tobacco. Many of the soldiers in camp had tobacco deposited in Richmond for sale. There was a rumor that British General Cornwallis was approaching Richmond. If Cornwallis captured Richmond then the tobacco would be lost to the owners.

James Blain realized this and hoped to buy the soldier's tobacco for a greatly reduced price. The soldiers in camp believed that Blain offering to purchase their tobacco was too low, and he was trying to take advantage of them. They took Blain into custody, called a court martial to hear his case, and found him guilty. For punishment they put him on his horse with his face toward the horse's tail, led him through camp, and sent him on his way.

Source: 1. Pension Application of George Duncan W9845.

My Pants Betrayed Me

Lewis Field entered the army in the middle of 1779 at the age of sixteen. He served in the Illinois Regiment under George Rogers Clark. His regiment fought Indians, and on June 6, 1780 he was captured by the Indians after a fight. He said he was running from several Indians when a strap of his "pantaloons caught a snag," and he fell down and was forced to surrender. Lewis was taken to the Indian camp and was tied to the stake to be burned alive. One of the Indian chiefs by the name of Little Turtle intervened and saved his life. He tells an interesting story in his pension application about his 3 year captivity with another man he calls Mr. Butts,

"Me together with Butts were rapidly marched on to the Maumee town at the mouth of Eel River on the Wabash. Here I after as before stated having been preserved by Little Turtle was adopted in to an Indian family & kindly treated until the fall of the year, when I was taken to Detroit where partly by force & partly by purchase the British under the command of Maj

Dupeister got him from the Indians, & at this Place I first saw the famous or rather infamous Simon Girty."

Simon Girty first sided with the colonists, and later switched sides and served with the Tories and their Indian allies. He was considered a renegade and turncoat, and was called "The White Savage" by the colonists.

Lewis continues in his application, *"Here every imaginable overture failing to induce him to enlist in the Kings service he together with seven other Prisoners – Cuthbert Steele, John Angel, Stephen Shelton, William Brooks, David Brooks, Ephraim Noel, Thomas Mehan & several other prisoners whose names I do not now recollect were put on board a schooner & sent down Lake Erie to Fort Shulier – and from there were marched down to the falls of Niagara. From here by water to Fort Niagara. Here we were put on Board of the British Ship of War Seneca mounting 26 Guns The Captains name I cannot recollect, but one of the Lieutenants was named Norvell. From Here I was taken to Carletons Island & Landed."*

"From Here we went on board of Battax through the Long Saut and on to Lashene. Here we Landed and marched to Montreal & were immediately put in Prison where i remained through the rigors of that Northern Clime miserably fed even eating Poor Canadian horses. Nearly twelve months when in consequence of the trouble given the British provision ships by the french fleet we were all like to starve to save them from which we were turned out among the farmers but as soon as spring came in consequence of some endeavoring to make our escape they we all handcuffed & again thrown into Prison."

"In the fall I cannot state the month Precisely we were marched up to and put upon Cote de Lake Island in the St. Lawrence. On this Island I remained until the next fall or about twelve months when by order of Sir Guy Carlton we were marched back to Montreal Put aboard of small vessels & sent to Quebec, where we remained in an almost starving condition eight weeks. Here I together with some 4 or 500 others were put on board a large old line of Battle ship commanded by Capt Yong out which the Guns had been taken and sailed for Philidelphia but were driven by stress of weather to anchor at the Isle of Beek. When the Gale increasing the ship commenced dragging her anchors."

"They got up two but the cable of the third had to be cut & the ship drove through the straights at the rate of thirteen knots an hour & for two weeks the gale drove them at this rate right out towards the west Indies when the wind shifted & after a voyage of forty days they off the Capes of Delware heard the report of Cannon ahead and presently saw the topsails of a ship & in a few minutes three other ships the first of which proved to be the South Carolina 60 gun ship said to be a present from Holland to the State of South Carolina Loaded with flower. The other three were British frigates I think two forty fours & a thirty six. The forty fours one on each side of the S.C. & the 36 under her stern. The Commander of one of the 44s hailed & commanded the Prison ship to follow him. after giving one Broadside the South Carolina struck her colours. And the ship of which I was on board ordered into New York instead of Philadelphia – where we Laid eight days."

"From there they saled up the North River thirty miles to Dobbs Ferry, and there we (the Prisoners) were delivered up to Col. Smith who commanded on the line on the Last day of Dec. 1782 who after taking a list of our names on the same day set us all at Liberty. From Dobbs Ferry I went to Philedelphia & thence in Feb 1783 he reached home in Culpepper County Va."

Source: 1. Pension Application S30413.

Beware of Africans Bearing Strawberries

The Americans employed many spies during the war, and one of them preformed a very spectacular deed. Pompey was an African slave that volunteered to spy for the American Army. The Americans had just lost Stony Point, New York in May of 1779. As a result Fort Fayette had fallen, West Point was in danger, and all communication to the north was threatened.

Pompey went to the fort at Stony Point with a basket of strawberries and he asked the sentry for permission to enter the fort and sell his fruit. The sentry saw no harm in letting in the laughing and harmless Pompey into the fort. The British officers, who were eager for fresh fruit quickly bought all that Pompey had. They insisted that he return with more, so for the next three days he sold his strawberries to the officers.

The third day he told the officers that he could not come back because he had to work. The officers were unhappy about this, so Pompey agreed to come after dark with the strawberries. To do this he said he needed to know the password, and the unsuspecting officers were happy to share it with him. Each night there was a new password, and for the next nine nights Pompey showed up with his strawberries and gave the password.

On the 10th night around midnight Pompey gave the password and the gates were opened. Only this time Pompey had with him three soldiers with blackened faces hiding by him. When the gates opened, they jumped out of hiding and knocked out the sentry. Other American troops were hiding, and they rushed inside the gates and more American troops scaled the back walls of the fort.

The British were taken completely by surprise and Stony Point was recaptured by the Americans. Pompey for his role in the victory was given a horse and excused from all work for the rest of his life.

Source: 1. American Revolution and War of 1812, Vol. 1.

How Much to Just Reach the Wall?

At the Battle of Stony Point Washington decided to encourage his men to capture the fort. He said the first man to enter the fort would receive a bounty of $500.00, the second man $400.00, the third man $300.00, the fourth $200.00, and the fifth $100.00. Around midnight the Americans stormed and captured the fort.

The bounty offered by General Washington was paid. Lt. Colonel Fleury was the first to enter the fort, and he personally tore down the British flag. He was followed by Lt. Knox, then Sergeant Baker of the Virginia line, Sergeant Spencer, and Sergeant Donlop. Each of the Sergeants received multiple wounds.

Sources: 1. *The Storming of Stony Point* by Donald N. Moran. 2. *The Enterprise in Contemplation: The Midnight Assault of Stony Point* by Donald Loprieno. 3. *The Storming of Stony Point on the Hudson* by Henry Phelps Johnston.

When I Say No Noise I Mean It

The Battle of Stony Point took place on July 16, 1779. The British commanded a fort on top of a hill at Stony Point, New York. General George Washington devised a plan to take the fort by attacking it at midnight with a little over 1,300 troops. This was not enough men to capture the heavily fortified British fort. However, Washington felt it could be achieved if they took the British by surprise, at midnight, and while clouds covered the moon.

Strict silence had to be maintained during the advance up the hill toward the fort. To ensure this silence Washington had the dogs in the area killed to prevent any barking as his men advanced toward the hill. To prevent an accidental firing of a musket the men were ordered not to load their weapons and use only bayonets.

Jane Moore filed for a widow's pension in 1840 and she stated in the application that her husband David told her, *"he was at the battle of Stony Point which she remembers more the more particularly, as he stated that they were made to go into battle with unloaded guns, which made him suspect that he together with his comrades had been sold."*

The men were also told that if during the approach to the fort they spoke or attempted to load their muskets they would be put to death. One American officer later reported that one man disobeyed the order, *"The column was ascending the hill. The man left his station and was loading his musket. I ordered him to return and desist from loading his musket. He refused, saying he did not understand fighting without firing. I immediately ran him through the body."*

Sources: 1. *The Storming of Stony Point* by Donald N. Moran, website. 2. *The Enterprise in Contemplation: The Midnight Assault of Stony Point*. 3. *The Storming of Stony Point on the Hudson* by Henry Phelps Johnston. 4. *The Untold Story of an Elite Regiment Who Changed the Course of the Revolution* by Patrick O'Donnell. 5. *Military Journal during the American Revolution from 1775 to 1783* by Dr. James Thacher, 1823. 6. Pension Application W1456 of David Moore filed by Jane Moore. 7. *The Storming of Stony Point - A Brief History of the United States*, Barnes's Historical Series, American Book Company, New York, 1885.

True Love

Sally St. Clair was a young dark-eyed creole girl at the time of the Revolutionary War. Sometime just before or near the beginning of the war William Jasper had saved her life. Jasper joined the 2nd South Carolina Regiment as a sergeant and marched off to war. Sally's gratitude to William for saving her life turned to love, which she kept secret from him. William had a lover in

Pennsylvania who, after he became a sergeant, he could afford to bring to South Carolina and marry.

Sally cut her hair and disguised her appearance so that she could pass for a young boy and followed William into the army. William was unaware that the young soldier was Sally. She stayed as near William as she could during her time in the army and no one suspected of her being a woman. Many times at night she would gaze upon William as he slept.

Sally and her secret love, William both fought at the Siege of Savannah in the fall of 1779. She and William both die on October 9, 1779 during the battle. Sally's secret was discovered when her body was prepared for burial. George Pope Morris wrote a poem about Sally that begins:

> In the ranks of Marion's band,
> Through morass and wooded land,
> Over beach of yellow sand,
> Mountain, plain and valley;
> A southern maid, in all her pride,
> March'd gayly at her lover's side,
> In such disguise
> That e'en his eyes
> Did not discover Sally.

Sources: 1. *The Revolutionary War* by Charles Patrick Neimeyer, page 88. 2. *The Romance of the Revolution: being a History of the Personal Adventures, Romantic Incidents, and Exploits Incidental to the War of Independence*, pages 323-5. 3. *The Deserted Bride: and Other Poems* by George Pope Morris, pages 87-88. 4. *Thrilling Adventures among the Early Settlers* by Warren Wildwood, pages 78-81.

The Legend of the Swamp Fox

Francis Marion was the leader of a group of militiamen in South Carolina during the Revolutionary War. His men served without pay, supplied their own horses, weapons, and many times they supplied their own food. He was hunted by the British and avoided capture by hiding out in swamps. He earned his nickname "Swamp Fox" from British Colonel Banastre Tarleton.

On one occasion Tarleton was in pursuit of Marion, when the cagey American escaped into the Ox swamp. Tarleton stopped the pursuit at the edge of the swamp and told his men, *"Come, my boys! Let us go back. We will soon find the Game Cock (meaning General Sumter), but as for this damned Swamp Fox, the devil himself could not catch him*

Marion is considered to be one of the fathers of modern guerrilla warfare. He is credited to later giving rise to the United States Rangers and other types of Special Forces. Marion's type of warfare during the Revolution was considered by the British to be very irregular.

In one skirmish Marion defeated British Colonel Watson, who had orders to hold an important bridge. When Watson surrendered his command to Marion he remarked, *"Why sir, you must certainly command a horde of savages, who delight in nothing but murder. I can't cross a swamp or a bridge, but I am waylaid and shot at as if I were a mad dog. Even my sentries are fired at and killed on their posts. Why, my god, sir! This is not the way that Christians ought to fight."*

Marion was quick to reply, *"I am sorry to be obliged to say, that from what I had known of them, the British officers were the last men on earth who had any right to preach about honor and humanity. That for men to come three thousand miles to plunder and hang innocent people, and then to tell that people how they ought to fight, betrayed an ignorance and impudence which he fain would hope had no parallel in the history of man. That for my part, I always believed, and still do believe that I should be doing God and his country good service to surprise and kill such men, while they continued this diabolical warfare, as I would the wolves and panthers of the forest."*

Francis Marion would have been captured in March of 1780 had it not been for a broken ankle he received, when he jumped out of a window at a party. At that time Marion was dining at the house of Mr. Alexander M'Queen in Charleston, South Carolina. The host of the party had locked all the doors for protection from the British and began to make countless toasts. Marion, who was not a man who enjoyed drinking, began to feel trapped. Marion discovered that the only way out of the house was to jump from the second story dining room window. Out the window he went, which cost him a broken ankle.

Since he was now unfit for duty, he decided to leave Charleston and heal his ankle in the countryside. As a result, he was not captured with the rest of the American Army in Charleston by the British.

Sources: 1. *The Life of General Francis Marion a Celebrated Partisan Officer in the Revolutionary War Against the British and Tories in South Carolina and Georgia* by Brig. Gen. P. Horry, pages 72-74 and 176-178. 2. *Heroes and Patriots of the South* by Cecil B. Hartley, pages 111-112. 3. *The Life of Francis Marion* by W. Gilmore Simms, pages 151-152.

Just a Small Prayer

When Charleston, South Carolina was attacked by the British they demanded that John Nicholas Martin the pastor of St. John's Lutheran Church pray for the king. He refused, so they banned the preacher from the city, confiscated his property, and shelled his church.

Source: 1. D.A.R. Lineage Book, Vol147, page 170.

Don't Worry, They Are Not Loaded

Charleston, South Carolina was captured by the British on May 12, 1780, and the American Army defending the town was captured. When the Americans were taken prisoner, their muskets were brought to the powder magazine inside the city. The Hessian officer in charge told his men that some of the muskets might still be loaded. Some of his men paid no attention to his warning and put loaded muskets in with the powder kegs. One of the muskets that was stacked fell and fired and it ignited 180 barrels of powder. It has been estimated that when it happened, it caused hundreds of other muskets to go off. Nearly 200 hundred people were killed including thirty British soldiers.

Sources: 1. *A Gallant Defense: The Siege of Charleston, 1780* by Carl P. Borick. 2. *An Account of the Siege of Charleston, South Carolina, in 1780* by General Wilmot DeSaussure, 1885.

But Don't Pass Notes in School

It was not uncommon for children to be used as spies against the British during the war. In 1780 the British had captured Charleston, South Carolina and watched very closely who entered the city. Mrs. Thomson, a patriot, obtained permission from British officers for herself and her little daughter Charlotte to enter the city. In one of the businesses she left Charlotte in a room, and told her that a gentleman or two might enter the room, but that she must not be frightened. She explained that the man might place something in her bosom, but not to be frightened by him.

While Charlotte was alone in the room a gentleman entered, looked around, bowed to the little girl, and put a folded paper into her bosom. He then left without saying a word. The mother returned and the two left the city at once. They later were conducted to the camp of American General Greene'.

The little girl was asked by the General, if she had something for him. Charlotte had forgotten about the note that was passed to her and told the General no. General Greene then asked her for the paper that had been put into her bosom, and she gave it to him. The note contained a description of British troops in Charleston.

Sources: 1. *Traditions and Reminiscences Chiefly of the American Revolution in the South* by Joseph Johnson, 1851, pages 102-103.

Who Turned Out the Lights?

"In four or five days after the Dark Day in the month of May 1780 Reuben Brooks then residing at Cambridge was drafted into the Service of the United States for the Term of three months in the company Commanded by Captain Woodford & Lieutenant North, Ensigns name do not recollect, one of the Sergeants name was Bowen & the Col or Generals name was Parsons—I preformed Service in said Company at New Haven in said State until the latter part of the Month of August 1780—when I was—discharged."

The "dark day" that Reuben refers to occurred on May 19, 1780 in the sky over New England. On that day there was unusual darkening of the sky. Several days prior to the 19th the sky had turned a dirty, yellowish color. When the darkness began around noon of the 19th, animal life reacted. Birds sang their evening songs and then went silent, chickens returned to their roosts, cattle began to return to their barns, and it became necessary to light candles in the homes. The cause may have been a combination of smoke from forest fires, thick fog, and cloud cover.

It caused a panic in the Connecticut Senate Chamber. Abraham Davenport arose and said, *"If it is not the Day of Judgment there is no reason to adjourn; if it is I prefer to be found doing my duty; bring in candles."*

Sources: 1. *New England's Dark Day* from the Weather Doctor Almanac, 2004. 2. U.S. Pension Roll of 1835. 3. Sons of the American Revolution Application. 4. Chapter Sketches, Connecticut D.A.R. Patriots' Daughters, 1900.

At Least my Leg is Still a Hero

General Benedict Arnold was one of George Washington's favorite Generals, and a hero at the Battle of Saratoga. During this battle Arnold was rallying his men, when his horse was hit in one of the final volleys in the battle. Arnold's leg was broken by both a musket ball and the horse falling on his leg. It was the same leg that was shot in an earlier battle. This left him crippled for a long period of time.

After Benedict Arnold turned traitor in 1780, he went from hero to one of the most hated men in America. He joined the British army, and during one expedition he asked a patriot captain, who had been taken prisoner, what he thought the Americans would do with him, if he should fall into their hands. The officer replied, "They will cut off the leg, which was wounded when you were fighting for the cause of liberty, and bury it with honors of war, and hang the rest of your body on a gibbet."

Source: 1. The Library of American Biography Vol. III, 1835 by Jared Sparks, page 322.

Take a Little Off the Top Please

Frederick Visscher was a Colonel of the 3rd Regiment of Tyron County Militia during the Revolutionary War. Frederick had sent his wife and child to Schenectady for safety because Tories had threatened to attack the area where Frederick lived. Tories were civilians that took up arms in support of the British. This deep hatred between Tories and Patriots pitted neighbor against neighbor and at times one family member against another.

Around 1780 British authorities would in some areas pay Indians and Tories between five and eight pounds for the scalp of an enemy. On Sunday night May 21, 1780, Sir John Johnson led 500 British Tories and Indians against the settlement where Colonel Frederick Visscher lived. Johnson divided his forces and sent a group, mostly Indians, to the area where Frederick lived. After burning some houses they reached the home of Frederick.

Inside the large house was Frederick, his mother, two brothers, and two sisters. The two sisters escaped from the cellar to the nearby woods. After a fight, the Indians gained entrance and Frederick's mother was hit on the head by a musket butt and tied to a chair. The two brothers were shot dead downstairs.

Frederick was hit in the head with a tomahawk, and then the Indian took the crown scalp from Frederick's head. The Indian turned Frederick over to cut his throat. Frederick wore a thick cravat around his throat and it prevented the knife from cutting the skin. The cravat was also red, so the Indian left him thinking he had cut his neck and Frederick was dead.

The Indians plundered the house and set it on fire. Frederick came to after the Indians left and drug the chair his mother was tied to outside the house. Frederick was treated for his injuries and recovered. He later had a silver plate fitted over part of his head to cover the wound from the scalping.

Frederick was very self-conscious of his missing scalp. He kept out of public view as much as he could. He even refused to attend a dinner in Schenectady, where General Washington was the honored guest. He finally consented to go and, was seated on the right side of Washington. The side with the missing scalp was away from the General.

Sources: 1. *Hudson-Mohawk Genealogies and Family Memories, Vol. 1.* by Cuyler Reynolds. 2. D.A.R. Lineage Book, Vol. 8, page 309.

Let's Liberate the Rum Kegs

An American regiment led by Colonel Thomas Sumter was sent on a campaign to harass or destroy a British outpost in South Carolina. The two sides met at Hanging Rock on August 6, 1780 and fought a three hour battle without pause on a very hot day. The Americans were unable to completely destroy the British, because they lacked enough ammunition and many men began to pass out from the excessive heat. The British lost 192 men and the Americans loss was only twelve. One group of American troops came across a storage of British rum and paused in the fighting to help themselves to the rum. They became so drunk they could not rejoin the battle and had to return to their camp.

Sources: 1. *Publications of the Southern History Association Vol. 1* by Colyer Meriwether. 2. Pension Papers of James McCaw S18117. 3. *A Guide to the Battles of the American Revolution* by Savas and Dameron.

Well Since You Put It That Way

John Murphy was taken prisoner by the British at the Battle of Camden in August of 1780, and for the next three weeks he was kept at Camden Jail. He wife visited the jail and begged for his release. He was given a parole after repeating the following to his captors, *"I John Murphy of Fishing Creek acknowledge myself a prisoner on parole to a detachment of his Majesty's troops under the command of the right Honorable Lieutenant General Earle [sic] of Cornwallis and I do promise that I will not act directly or indirectly against his Majesty's Government nor stir up others so to do, that I will not speak or say anything that shall be prejudicial to his Majesty's interest and will confine myself to my own plantation not exceeding one mile from thence until further enlarged."*

After his release Murphy went to the camp of American General Sumter who told him that no good man and patriot would be bound by such a promise. So Murphy tore up his parole and joined the army under command of Captain John Henderson.

Source: Pension application of John Murphy S7260.

Of Course I Know You

During the Battle of Musgrove Mill on August 19, 1780 one of the Tory commanders, Colonel Daniel Clary, mounted his horse to escape. Two patriot militiamen seized the bridle bit of the horse to stop his escape. Because there was confusion and the militias on both side were not in uniforms, Colonel Clary yelled out, *"Damn you, don't you know your own officers?"* He was quickly released and allowed to escape.

Source: 1. *Traditions and Reminiscences Chiefly of the American Revolution in the South* by Joseph Johnson, 1851, page 488.

What's Your Best Offer?

History books record the story of the capture of Major John Andre, who was the famous British spy. Andre had negotiated with American General Benedict Arnold the capture of West Point in exchange for money and a commission in the British army for Arnold. Arnold later fled in disgrace and Andre was hung as a spy. So how did Andre get captured in the first place?

Isaac Van Wart, John Paulding, and David Williams, who were all around twenty years old were in the local militia. They were on morning guard duty on September 23, 1780 when they stopped John Andre not knowing he was a British officer.

Major Andre was a British officer and spy. Benedict Arnold had provided Andre with civilian cloths and a passport so that Andre could escape back to British lines. Andre carried hidden papers in Arnold's handwriting, which showed the British how to capture West Point. Around nine in the morning Andre approached the three young sentries. Andre thought they were Tories because Pauling was wearing a Hessian soldier's overcoat. Pauling had stolen the coat when he had escaped from Tories while visiting his girlfriend. The spy told the boys that he must not be detained, because he was a British officer on a mission.

The boys took Andre prisoner, but Andre said he was an American officer and showed them his fake passport. The boys were now very curious, so they searched him and found the incriminating papers. As luck would have it, Paulding was the only one of the three boys that could read. Andre bribed the boys by offering them his watch and horse if they would let him go. The boys told him that if he was a British officer he could do more. Andre then pulled out a purse of gold. The boys then told Andre that he could not tempt them into releasing him.

They turned down the lucrative offer and took him to their headquarters. Because of the boy's heroic efforts, Andre was hung as a spy. Benedict Arnold was removed from the army as a traitor, and West Point was saved.

Later with the recommendation of George Washington, Congress awarded the three boys a silver medal, a federal pension of $200 a year, and they were given nice farms by the state of New York. All three boys survived the war and lived long lives.

Sources: 1. *The Traitor and the Spy: Benedict Arnold and John Andre* by James Thomas Flexner. 2. *Journal or Historical Recollections of American Events during the Revolutionary War* by Elias Boudinot, 1894.

A Traitor to Catch a Traitor

Everyone has heard the story of the traitor Benedict Arnold. He was an American General who at the start of his career was a hero and later turned villain. He offered to turn over the fort at West Point to the British in exchange for money and a command in the British Army. His plan was discovered and Arnold escaped capture by the Americans and joined the British Army.

Washington felt betrayed by Arnold and hungered to capture him. Washington told Major Henry Lee that he wanted Arnold brought back alive in order to *"make a public example of him."* Lee devised a plan to send an American soldier posing as a traitor to join the camp where Arnold was, befriend him, capture him, and bring him to the American lines.

Lee chose a man for the mission that he knew, John Champe. On October 20, 1780 Champe left the American camp to board a boat to take him to New York City. Once in New York Champe was taken by the British and interrogated for several days. They were finally satisfied that his story of desertion was true and said that they wanted him to join their army. He was assigned to the force comprised mainly of American born troops commanded by Benedict Arnold. Champe talked with Arnold, who was impressed with his background and story. Arnold had him stay with his troops as a recruiter, which now gave Champe access to Arnold.

Every evening Arnold would take a walk in the garden behind his home. The garden was concealed by a fence and near the river. The plan was to abduct Arnold while he walked in the garden, remove a board in the fence, and take him through the opening and down to the river to a waiting boat. If anyone saw his taking Arnold to the river, he would tell them he was taking a drunk officer to his barracks. Champe had an assistant to help him with the abduction of Arnold. Mr. Baldwin had been offered money, five hundred acres of land, and three slaves for his assistance in the kidnapping.

It was a great plan, but before it could be carried out Arnold and his men were ordered out of New York City and sent to Virginia. Champe went with the army, and he even fought with them for several weeks. When he saw there was no chance to capture Arnold, he deserted and made his way back to American lines. He wanted to continue to fight the British, but Washington felt he should be discharged from the service. Washington told Champe that if he was captured by the British he would be hanged as a spy. Champe left the army and returned to his home.

Sources: 1. *Revolutionary War Amid Southern Chaos* by George W. Hicks. 2. *A Military Journal during the American Revolutionary War from 1775 to 1783* by James Thacher.

The Mailbox in the Cupboard

Sarah Townsend lived in Oyster Bay, Long Island. Her brother Robert was a spy for General George Washington, who was working under the pseudonym of "Culper Junior" in the famous Culper spy ring. During the Revolutionary War, her house was occupied by Colonel John Simcoe of the British army.

One day Sarah saw a strange man in her kitchen, who placed a letter in the cupboard, and then left the house. She got the letter and saw it was addressed to John Anderson, and she looked at the contents which meant nothing to her. She did not know that John Anderson was the pseudonym for British Major John Andre. She later saw Andre go to the cupboard and take the letter.

That evening she overheard a conversation between Andre and Simcoe and she heard the words "West Point." Knowing that this could be important since West Point was an important American fort, she sent a message to her brother Robert. Sarah did not know that General Benedict Arnold was planning on turning over West Point to the British.

Robert informed General Washington of what Sarah had seen and heard. Later Andre was captured and the plans to capture West Point were exposed. In a small way Sarah had saved West Point.

Sources: 1. *Gallantry in Action: A Biographic Dictionary of Espionage in the American Revolutionary War* by Harry Mahoney and Marjorie Locke Mahoney. 2. *Women Patriots of the American Revolution: a Biographical Dictionary* by Charles E. Claghorn.

They Should Have Taught the Horses to Tiptoe

At the Battle of Black Mingo on September 14, 1780 Americans under the command of Colonel Francis Marion, "The Swamp Fox", tried to surprise a group of Loyalist troops under the command of Colonel Ball. Sometime after midnight the Americans had their surprise attack spoiled, when the lead horses crossed the wooden plank bridge across Black Mingo Creek. The noise of the hooves alerted the Loyalist troops and the battle began. The Loyalists were disorganized, and in fifteen minutes the battle was over when the enemy retreated into the swamp.

Both sides were so close together in the battle that pieces of wadding from their guns struck on each other when fired. The Americans captured guns, ammunition, barrage, and horses. Colonel Marion took Loyalists Colonel John Ball's horse for himself and renamed it Ball. Colonel Marion learned from the battle to never cross a bridge at night in a surprise attack, without spreading blankets on the bridge to muffle the hooves of the horses.

Colonel Francis Marion

Sources: 1. *The Swamp Fox: Lessons in Leadership from the Partisan Campaigns of Francis Marion* by Scott Aiken. 2. *The Life and Times of General Francis Marion* by Horatio Newton Moore, pages 60-70.

Don't Mess With This Family

Fourteen year old Zaccheus Wilson had six brothers and a father that also served during the revolution. His brothers Robert and Joseph were taken prisoners at the surrender of Charleston and were later allowed to return home. Once at home rather than be forced to join the Tory militia they enlisted again in the American army. In one battle Joseph encountered a Tory militiaman that he knew in hand-to-hand combat. He killed the Tory after a severe struggle and carried off the dead man's rifle. Zaccheus's father Robert and his brother John were later captured and placed in jail in Camden. One of their jail mates was Andrew Jackson, the future president.

In October of 1780 General Cornwallis and his troops stopped at the Wilson plantation and began stealing provisions. Cornwallis soon learned that he was at the home of a patriot leader who had seven sons in the rebel army. Cornwallis encouraged Mrs. Wilson to have her husband and sons join the British army. He offered them rank, honor, and wealth if they joined.

Mrs. Wilson replied, *"I have seven sons who are now, or have been bearing arms. Indeed my seventh son, Zaccheus, who is only fifteen years old, I yesterday assisted to get ready to go and join his brothers in Sumter's army. Now sooner than see one of my family turn back from the glorious enterprise, I would take these boys* [pointing to three or small sons] *and with them would myself enlist under Sumter's standard, and show my husband and sons how to fight, and if necessary to die for their country."*

The cruel Lieutenant Colonel Banastre Tarleton turned to General Cornwallis and sneered, *"Ah! General! I think you've gotten into a hornet's nest! Never mind, when we get to Camden, I'll take good care that old Robert Wilson never comes back again!"* He apparently knew that Robert Wilson was in jail at Camden.

The next day the British army moved out, and a group of scouts captured Zaccheus who was found on the flank of the British with his rifle. It appeared that he was preparing to lie in wait and ambush some of the enemy. He was taken to Cornwallis, who demanded that the boy act as a guide. He wanted the young boy to show him the best place to cross the Catawba River. When the British reached the river, Zaccheus showed them the best place to cross. Some of the British troops were half way across, when they found themselves in deep water and were swept down river by the strong current.

Cornwallis, red with rage, drew his sword and said he was going to cut the boy's head off for his treachery. Zaccheus faced him and replied, *"I have no arms and I am your prisoner. You have the power to kill me."* He then added, *"But Sir, don't you think it would be a cowardly act for you to strike an unarmed boy with your sword. If I had but half of your weapon, it would not be so cowardly, but then you know you would not be so safe."* If this exchange had taken place between Zaccheus and Colonel Tarleton, the young boy would have likely been killed on the spot.

Cornwallis realizing that he was not acting the part of a gentleman and also impressed with the lad's courage said to him, *"You are a fine fellow, and I would not hurt a hair on your head. Go home and take care of your mother and tell her to keep her boys at home."*

Later sometime in November Cornwallis ordered that Robert, his son John, and several other men be released from jail in Camden and had them safely transported to a prison in Charleston. Before the guards arrived, Robert organized the men to escape. When the prisoners overpowered their guards, Robert Wilson made the guards swear never again to bear arms against the rebels and sent them on their way with a warning, *"If I ever find a single mother son of you in arms again, I will hang you up to a tree like a dog."* With people like the Wilsons it is no wonder that the rebels won their freedom from Great Britain.

Sources: 1. *Women of the Revolution, Vol. III, Chapter XX, 1852* by Elizabeth F. Ellett. 2. *Women of the Frontier* by Billy Kennedy. 3. *Women of the Century* by Phebe Ann Hannaford. 4. Will of Zaccheus Wilson.

Betrayed by His Left Hand

Major Patrick Ferguson was a Scottish officer in the British Army, and he led the Loyalist militia against the Patriot militia at the battle of Kings Mountain on October 7, 1780. It was a very bloody battle, because the Patriots were seeking revenge for the killing of militiamen by British Colonel Banastre Tarleton at the Battle of Waxhaws. Tarleton's men killed many Americans as they tried to surrender.

Battle of Waxhaws

The Patriot militiamen were not sure what Major Ferguson looked like until they received a tip from a local woman. The pension application statement of John McQueen (McQuin), who was present at the battle, provided insight on how Ferguson was identified.

"There was a woman who Ferguson had been keeping who had left the British army and had come to Capt. Lewis and she told him that Ferguson could be known by him using his sword in his left hand as he had been wounded previously in the right and Capt. Lewis communicated this to Col. Cleveland and after the battle commenced, he pointed out Ferguson and selected 8 or 9 of his best riflemen and told them he had to fall, and there was 6 or 7 bullet holes through him after the battle."

Source: 1. Pension Application S30577.

Stories from the Battle of Kings Mountain, October 7, 1780

At times the war in the south became a bitter struggle between neighbors and families. The Battle of Kings Mountain, a Patriot victory, was fought between the Patriots and Tories, and was one of the bloodiest battles fought in the Revolution. The savagery in battles between the Patriots and Tories in battles even shocked the British and Hessian troops. Relatives, friends, and neighbors fought against each other during this battle. The Tories had 290 men killed, 163 wounded, and 668 captured. The following are a few strange stories that occurred during the battle.

Patriot Thomas Robertson was hiding behind a tree, when a Tory neighbor saw him and called him by name. When Robertson peeped around the tree to see who had called him, the Tory fired and barely missed him. Robertson quickly fired back and mortally wounded the sneaky Tory. The man yelled to Robertson, "Robertson, you have ruined me!" Robertson replied back, "The devil help you!"

Source: 1. *King's Mountain and Its Heroes: History of the Battle of King's Mountain, October 7th, 1780,* by Lyman C. Draper, page 265.

***

During the height of the battle, patriot William Twitty saw a friend shot dead by a Tory hiding behind a tree. William waited until his friend's killer exposed himself to take another shot. When William saw the Tory poke his head from behind of the tree, he fired and saw the man fall. After the battle he went back to the tree where the dead man laid, and he discovered that the man he had killed was one of his neighbors.

Source: 1. *King's Mountain and Its Heroes: History of the Battle of King's Mountain, October 7th, 1780,* by Lyman C. Draper, page 265.

***

One of the men, in patriot Major Hammond's command, was a man who proved himself in several battles to be a man of courage. The night before the Kings Mountain battle he had a premonition that he would be killed. The next day, before he reached the battle, he decided to save his life for future battles for his country, so he left the troops and hid himself. He was found and returned to his unit, and once again he found a way to leave and hide. Again he was found and taken to the front line. This time he decided to stay, and he took part in the battle. He was later found shot dead in the forehead. Upon hearing of the man's death, the Major, who had great respect for the man, regretted that he had not known of the circumstances, because he would have respected the soldier's desire to not take part in the battle.

Source: 1. *King's Mountain and Its Heroes: History of the Battle of King's Mountain, October 7th, 1780,* by Lyman C. Draper.

***

There were several doctors available to treat the injured men on both sides. The wounded could be found lying all around the battlefield and the sides of the mountain. One patriot Lieutenant was found wounded in the abdomen and was saved from dying, because he had very little to eat the past three days and his stomach was almost empty.

Source: 1. *King's Mountain and Its Heroes: History of the Battle of King's Mountain, October 7th, 1780,* by Lyman C. Draper.

***

When the shooting had ended, one of the men from South Carolina, who was noted to run at the first sound of battle, returned. Before the battle some of his friends, knew that when shots were fired he would get the urge to take to the hills, so they advised him to stay behind. "No," he replied, "I am determined to stand my ground today, live or die." When the first shot was fired, to the surprise of no one he took to his heels, and after the fight was over he returned. His friends began to give him "the business" for his conduct. He offered this excuse, "From the first fire, I knew nothing whatever till I was gone about a hundred and fifty yards; and when I came to myself, recollecting my resolves, I tried to stop; but my confounded legs would carry me off."

Source: 1. *King's Mountain and Its Heroes: History of the Battle of King's Mountain, October 7th, 1780,* by Lyman C. Draper, page 254-255.

***

A few days after the Battle of Kings Mountain, Colonel Campbell ordered a court martial to sit, which was composed of the Field Officers and Captains. He wanted trials for some of the Tories taken prisoner during the battle. These men were accused of crimes in the area before the battle took place. Witnesses were called, and each case was examined.

The trials lasted all day, and over thirty men were tried and found guilty. At six that evening they began to hang the convicted men three at a time. One of the crimes proven against a Captain, that was executed, was that he had called at the house of a Patriot inquiring if he was at home. He was informed by the Patriot's son, a small boy, that he was not, and the Captain immediately drew out his pistol and shot the boy.

When nine men had been hung, Colonel Shelby interfered and proposed that the hanging stop. The rest of the officers agreed, and the remaining guilty men were spared. One of the men that tried to stop the hangings was Colonel Elias Alexander, this author's 6th great uncle.

A spared and grateful prisoner whispered to Colonel Shelby, "You have saved my life, and I will tell you a secret. British Colonel Tarleton will be here in the morning. A woman has brought the news." The saved man was telling the truth, because Lord Cornwallis had detached Colonel Tarleton to pursue and attack the Patriots and to rescue the prisoners. This information saved the lives of many of the Patriots.

Source: 1. *King's Mountain and Its Heroes: History of the Battle of King's Mountain, October 7th, 1780,* by Lyman C. Draper, page 544.

***

During the battle, William Sharp saw his friend and cousin, William Giles, get shot in the neck and fall to the ground in a pool of blood. Sharp stopped for a moment, brushed away a tear from his eye, and said, "Poor fellow, he is dead, but I am spared a little longer, I will avenge him." After firing his rifle several times, he was astonished to see Giles raise up, rest on his elbow, and start loading his gun. Giles was soon upon his feet again, fought through the battle, and lived to a good old ripe age.

Source: 1. *King's Mountain and Its Heroes: History of the Battle of King's Mountain, October 7th, 1780,* by Lyman C. Draper, page 269.

***

John Fox fought at the Battle of Kings Mountain on October 7, 1780. Within half an hour he was wounded when a musket ball *"passed through the flesh of my left arm and into my left side which ball remains in me to this day."* The next day he was placed on a horse with a bundle of bedclothes on his saddle to lean on, and he was sent home. His journey home was nearly ninety miles.

Source: 1. Pension application R3734.

***

You Don't Play Fair

A strange battle took place on December 4, 1780 and no one was killed, wounded, and no shots were fired. It was called the Battle of Rugeley's Mills and the Americans were victorious.

It began when patriots trapped 115 Tories in Mr. Rugeley's house and barn. The Americans surrounded the place and demanded the surrender of the Tories. The Tories feeling they were fairly safe refused to surrender. Colonel William Washington, cousin to George Washington, told a couple of his men to get him a large log. The men found a large log and the Colonel had them paint it black. He mounted the painted log on another fallen log, and pointed it toward the house. He stood by his "cannon" and told the Tory leader that if they did not surrender he was going to blow them to pieces. Out marched 115 Tories and several British soldiers with their hands raised fooled by what is known as a "Quaker Gun." I suspect that all the men on both sides had a good belly laugh when it was learned that the Tories surrendered because of a log.

Francis Miller told about the incident in his pension application of 1834. *"In the autumn of 1780 I marched the company which I was Captain of at home from Mecklenburg to Rugeley's Mill, December 4, 1780. We met Col. Lee and Col. Washington and at the request of Col. Washington I made a wooden cannon about the size of a 6 pounder, this Cannon was drawn up in sight of the Fort in which were a British officer, seven privates, and a number of Tories, who being terrified at the sight of a wooden Cannon, threw open the gates, and surrendered without firing a gun."*

Sources: 1. *Military Journal during the American Revolution from 1775 to 1783* by Dr. James Thacher, 1823. 2. Pension Application W5673 of William Reed. 3. Pension Application W23984 of Francis Miller.

If You Want Something Done Right, Do It Yourself

In 1780 an American soldier was sentenced to hang for the crime of forging a number of discharges, by which he and more than a hundred soldiers had left the army. Before he was executed he addressed the soldiers telling them to be faithful to their country and obedient to their officers. He told the officers to be punctual in all their engagements to the soldiers and give them no cause to desert.

As he stood on the gallows he examined the rope to be used to hang him. He said the hangman knot was not made right, and the rope was not strong enough since he was such a heavy man. He adjusted the knot and placed it around his neck and was swung off at once. The rope broke, and he fell to the ground and was much bruised.

He calmly climbed back on the gallows and said, *"I told you the rope was not strong enough, do get me a stronger one."* They got another rope and proceeded to hang him.

Source: 1. *Military Journal during the American Revolution from 1775 to 1783* by Dr. James Thacher, 1823.

You Just Wait Until Our Momma Gets Here

Rosanna Farrow was proud that she had five sons old enough to fight for freedom in the Revolutionary War. Her husband had recently died from smallpox, and she was left with eight children to raise. Her boys, the oldest was not yet twenty-one, were in active service in 1780 when the British were trying to stamp out disloyalty to the king. Many times the prisoners taken by the British were shot soon after they were captured.

One night Rosanna was awakened by someone at her front gate. She asked who was there, and the stranger told her it was a friend with a message. She went down stairs to talk to the stranger and was told that three of her boys had been captured by the British and were in jail. She was then told that the British Colonel intended to shoot the prisoners before he left the area.

Rosanna told her girls to stay in the house, and she mounted their horse and rode off to the American camp. She met with the American Colonel and told him her story. The Colonel told her that the British would usually swap prisoners, so he gave her six British prisoners and a soldier to guard them. Taking no time to rest she rode off with the group to the British camp.

By daybreak she reached the British camp and sought out the commander, Colonel Cruger. She told him of the offer for exchange and he agreed and then added, *"Well, you are just in time, for I had given orders for those rebellious youngsters of yours to be hanged at sunrise, but I guess you can take the rebels."*

"My sons!" she said in anger. *"I have given you two for one, Colonel, but understand that I consider it the best trade I ever made, for rest assured hereafter the 'Farrow boys' will whip you four to one."*

As she marched off followed by her sons, one British soldier remarked with a half-smile, *"That's a pretty good speech for so dainty a lady, but she is as warm for the cause as the men."*

Sources: *1. Women Patriots of the American Revolution a Biographical Dictionary* by Charles E. Claghorn. 2. *Descendants and Related Families of David Samuel Ware and Amanda Roelee Chesteen* by Sarah Hazel Delgado. 3. D.A.R. Lineage Book, Vol 37, page 4.

Chapter 6
Victory and in Time Peace 1781-1783

"Oh god, it's all over." British Prime Minister Lord North when told of the defeat of General Cornwallis.

Things did not look well for the Americans at the start of 1781. The economy of the United States was in shambles. Mismanagement of money, excessive military spending, and counterfeit money spread by the British was in circulation. There was no money to pay most of the troops or wagon drivers to bring supplies. General Washington was in the north, and he believed that there must be an important military victory in 1781 or the war may yet be lost. There were even rumors that the French government might pull their support from the American cause. British General Clinton had shifted half his army to the north to New York City to keep Washington in check.

By mid-year events began to unfold that would change the course of the war. In the south General Nathanael Greene was playing a cat-and-mouse game with General Cornwallis. Greene continued to strike and withdraw while losing every battle. The Americans began to divide, elude, and tire the army of Cornwallis with these hit and run tactics. The British were eventually driven to Yorktown with their backs to the sea.

The British fleet was sent to Yorktown to aid Cornwallis and were driven off by the French fleet. In order to trap the British, Generals Greene and Lafayette would need many more soldiers. In New York General Washington gave up his plan to try to take New York City from the British. He leaked false information to British General Clinton to make him think that he was going to remain in New York. Instead, he led his men to Yorktown and joined his army with Lafayette's men. Cornwallis was now trapped and his men were under siege for nearly three weeks. On October 19, 1781 his army of over 8,000 troops were either killed, wounded, or captured.

Most people believe that the American Revolution ended with the capture of Cornwallis. The surrender at Yorktown turned the British public against the war, but the British military continued to fight. It would be another two years before American Independence was completed. There were still 30,000 British soldiers in America. They occupied New York City, Savannah, Canada, and parts of Florida. There were also pockets of Tory resistance particularly in New York, and the Indians would continue to be a problem as the Americans moved westward. General Washington now struggled to keep his army intact to face the remaining British in New York. Many of the French troops had returned home, and the American militia men returned to their farms and shops.

Instead of continuing the war in America, the British chose to put its dwindling resources toward fighting the French and Spain for control of Europe and to keep the remainder of the British Empire intact. The final peace treaty was signed in Paris in September 1783, and the last of the British army left New York City in November. What most people thought was impossible eight years earlier had now become reality.

Beau Geste

In 1781 South Carolina was overrun with British troops and their Tory allies. Charles Mackey was a patriot who led a band of men who fought with General Francis Marion. Charles was noted for being hard-headed, impulsive, and prone to taking unnecessary risks. His wife Lydia

Mackey was the opposite, being a woman of good common sense, a clear head, and sound judgement.

The Mackey home was about two miles from the camp of British Lt. Colonel Tarleton. He was well known as a vicious, cruel, and hateful officer. Because of the close proximity of the British camp, Charles knew it would be extremely dangerous for him to visit his home. But being an impulsive person, he left his camp and went home for a visit. During his visit he would go out at times to the British camp to gather information.

He would spend most of his days in a nearby swamp and visit his home at night. He had a watch dog that would bark loudly whenever anyone approached the farm. One evening while home the dog failed to sound an alarm when Tory riders approached. When they approached the house they yelled out, *"Hallo."* Mrs. Mackey jumped from her bed and looked out her second story window to see six armed men who were strangers.

She asked what they wanted and they said, *"Is Charlie Mackey at home?"* She replied that he was not, and while this conversation was taking place Charles was planning to escape the house. He was about to raise a loose plank in the floor, crawl under the house to the back, and then make his way through the orchard to the swamp. He had successfully used this escape route on several occasions.

The riders told Mrs. Mackey that there was a big fight yesterday between General Marion and the British, and that the British were defeated. They said they had been sent with orders to join General Marion at Lansford, and to attack Tarleton. They continued by saying, *"We do not know the way to Lansford, and have come to get Charlie to show us the way."*

The cautious Mrs. Mackey said she was sorry that her husband was not home to ride with them. Charles, hearing all of this and being impulsive, came out of the house and ran to the men shouting hurrahs for General Marion and vowing death to the British. The leader of the riders replied calmly, *"Well, Charlie, old fellow, we have set many traps for you, but never baited them right until now. You are our prisoner."* They bound him and rode off toward the camp of Tarleton. Once there he was tried and sentenced to death as a spy.

The next morning Mrs. Mackey figured that her husband would be taken to Tarleton's camp, so she gathered some fruit and eggs and rode to the camp. Once in the camp she met a young officer who told her that Colonel Tarleton was on parade and for her to take a seat.

Colonel Tarleton   National Archives

He asked her if she brought the eggs and fruit to sell. Lydia Mackey told the officer that she brought the food as a way to get to see Colonel Tarleton. She explained to the man that her husband was captured and wished to get him released, if he were still alive.

Again, she was told that the Colonel was on parade and would not return for at least two hours. Lydia, who could be rather charming, appealed to the softer side of the officer, who began to feel sorry for the woman. He said that he would prepare the papers for the release of her husband, and all Tarleton would have to do would be to sign the document. The officer, knowing that his Colonel was not noted for being understanding toward the desires of the Americans, told her that the Colonel probably would not sign it.

Around noon Colonel Tarleton, tall, handsome, and clean shaven rode up and entered his tent. The sympathetic officer told Lydia that the Colonel would have to dine first, before he would present the paper to him for a signature. Soon the Colonel came out of his tent and started to mount his horse. Lydia stepped forward and explained to him the purpose of her visit. The Colonel said he was in a hurry and could not help her at this time. Lydia explained that her husband had been condemned to death, and only the Colonel had the power to save him.

Tarleton brushed the woman off by saying, *"When I get back later in the day I'll look into it."* He then placed his foot in the stirrup and sprang up to mount his horse. Before he could throw his leg over, Lydia grabbed his coat and pulled him down. He turned to her in a fit of anger and said he would look into it when he returned. Again, he attempted to mount, and once more Lydia pulled him down begging him to spare her husband.

Tarleton was quite angry, for he had killed people for less than what this woman was doing. He said to her, *"Do you know what you are doing? I will attend to this at my convenience and not sooner."* He then turned to try to mount for the third time, and for the third time Lydia pulled him down. *

This time she held the scabbard of his sword and fell to her knees. She cried out, *"Draw your sword and slay me, or give me the life of my husband, for I will never let you go until you kill me or sign this document,"* which she held up before his face.

Tarleton was trembling with rage, because no colonial had ever dared to treat him this way. He called out to his officer, *"Captain, where is this woman's husband?"* Tarleton was told the prisoner was in a nearby tent. *"Order him to be brought here,"* the Colonel demanded. Charley Mackey was brought before the red-faced Colonel who said, *"Sir, you have been convicted of bearing arms against His Majesty's government; worse, you have been convicted of being a spy. You have dared to enter my lines in disguise as a spy, and you cannot deny it, but for the sake of your wife I will give you a full pardon on condition that you will take an oath never again to bear arms against the King's government."*

Now Charles Mackey was many things but dishonest was not among them. *"Sir,"* said Mackey, *"I cannot accept pardon on these terms. It must be unconditional or I must die."* Then poor Lydia also cried out, *"I, too, must die."* A shocked Tarleton turned to his Captain and paused before he spoke, *"Captain, for God's sake sign my name to this paper and let this woman go."* With that Tarleton was finally able to mount his horse, and he quickly rode off. This was probably the only nice gesture toward a colonial that Tarleton made during the entire Revolution.

Source: 1. *Revolutionary Reader, Reminiscences and Indian Legends* by Sophie Lee Foster, page, 88-93.

Funny, You Don't Look American

The Battle of Haw River, also known as Piles Defeat, occurred on a cold day on February 25, 1781 in North Carolina. Dr. John Pyle, the Tory commander, was riding along with his men when they came upon a column of mounted men. He mistakenly thought they were British troops under the command of Banastre Tarleton, who he knew was in the area. The troops were not British, but American.

It was dusk, and Tarleton's British troops and the American mounted troops both wore green uniforms. Two of Pyle's scouts rode up to the mounted troops. One scout rode back to Pyle to tell him they had found Tarleton, while the other scout engaged in conversation with the troop commander he believed to be the British commander. Soon the two opposing columns approached each other, and Pyle's column moved off the road in respect of what they thought were British dragoons.

The American troops under Colonel Lee rode past with their swords drawn in salute. Meanwhile, the American foot soldiers had moved off the road and taken up positions in the woods. As Colonel Lee approached Pyle in the rear of the column they exchanged greetings, and they were shaking hands when someone began shouting and soon musket shots were fired. Once the fighting started the Americans were prepared, since they already had their swords drawn. Pyle was knocked from his horse and asked for mercy. Within ten minutes the "battle" was over. The Tories had 90 men killed and 250 wounded. The American had one horse killed. This author is sure that the Americans that were there laughed about this "battle" for many years afterwards. This author doubts that many of the surviving Tories would ever admit being there.

Sources: 1. *The American Revolution in the Southern Colonies* by David Lee Russell. 2. North Carolina Genealogy Webpage. 3. Pension Papers S6834 of William Falls. 4. *A Guide to the Battles of the American Revolution* by Theodore P. Savas & J. David Dameron.

The Reason I Served

Bishop Tyler wanted to enlist at the age of twelve, but he could not get his father's permission. Just before he turned fourteen his father gave him permission to join and serve as a waiter and play the fife. Bishop was to serve with a family friend, Captain Charles Miles. The young boy enlisted on March 1, 1781 for one year into a company of state troops commanded by Captain Charles Miles.

After the war Bishop Tyler had several people write to the pension bureau to give proof of his service. For some reason he felt compelled to write a letter to the bureau on December 5, 1833 and explain why he joined the army at such a young age when he was not required to do so. It was a very moving and patriotic account given to Judge John Hyde, who wrote down what Bishop said.

"Bishop Tyler of the town of Griswold in the county of New London, being called to explain why a youth of the tender age of fourteen should be engaged in the service of his country, when the militia laws did not <u>require</u> those under sixteen years to be enlisted in the militia feels no small mortification at being called upon to answer <u>such a question</u> to obtain the small sum which the tardy justice of his country has seen fit bestow as testimony of its estimation of these services."

"But the question recurs, why <u>at the under age of fourteen,</u> he engages in the service of his country when the law did not oblige him to do so? The answers, because he loves his country.

Because he was born and educated in New England. In Connecticut in the Parish of Pachang in the town of Preston, In a Parish where he was accustomed to attend Public worship on the <u>Sabbath</u>, where the Parish Minister was an ardent friend of his country & taught his people to pray for the success of the righteous cause in which it was engaged, where the people at his recommendation on one Sabbath & information of the distresses of the soldiers of the revolution came laden on the next Sabbath with blankets, mittens, shoes, & stockings & other necessaries for their relief filled the broad aisles with them & which was dispatched for their use as soon as the Sabbath & its holy services had ended where Mothers, or one at least on helping her young son to pit on his knapsack to join the army, took him by the hand----bid him Adieu---prayed God to help & preserve him but charged him whatever might happen to him never to let her hear that he "died of a wound in his back."

"Because finally he was the son of Colonel Samuel Tyler a member of the same Parish & himself an officer of the revolution: liberty, and finally yielded to the importunity of a son whose juvenile order had been unkindled by his own spirit to take part in avenging its wrongs----If more be necessary, he adds, that he well recollects when he was twelve years old a company of soldiers Commanded by Capt. Carr were passing from Rhode Island to join the continental army tarried at his father's house one nighty and noticed him playing on a fife made from a stalk of elder bush & urged him to enlist as his fifer, he agreed to do so, if his father's consent could be obtained it was applied for & refused, but from that time he continually importuned his father to enlist, to which he finally consented when he could place him under the charge & as the waiter of his friend & neighbor Capt. Charles Miles with whom he served as stated in his original declaration and before that service expired had occasion to use other weapons than a fife & preform other service that those of a waiter to his captain who was a prisoner to the enemy."

Sources: 1. Tombstone. 2. Pension Papers S30377. Connecticut Town Marriage Records pre-1870. 3. U.S. Pensioners 1818-1872. 4. U.S. Revolutionary War Rolls 1775-1783.

A Promise Made, A Promise Kept

John Davenport grew up in Virginia and he was an honest, truthful, and obedient boy. In the same county was another boy, Harry Burnley, who was also a young boy of high character. John and Harry were great friends and hunted, fished, and played together as they grew up.

In 1772 John married Lucy Barksdale, a sixteen year old girl of great beauty. The young couple spent many happy days together, and they began to raise a family. When the Revolution began John Davenport and his life-long friend Harry Burnley joined the fight together. Over the years they were engaged in many battles.

On the night of March 14, 1781 the two boys were with the army encamped at Guilford Court House, North Carolina. That evening they were preparing for the battle the next day. John approached Harry and sadly said, *"Harry, somehow I feel that I will be killed in battle tomorrow. I almost know it."* Harry tried to cheer up John by laughing and making light of John's premonition. Harry finally said, *"John, if you are killed tomorrow, I am going back home and marry your widow."* Harry, a young man, had never married.

The next day the battle was fought and many men were left dead or dying on the bloody battlefield. One of the wounded men suffering from both pain and thirst was John Davenport. When his life-long friend Harry found him, scavengers were stripping John's body of his silver buckles which he wore. Harry chased the men away and began to give water to his dying friend.

Realizing that his time was near, John said to his friend, *"Harry, I am dying; and you remember last night you said to me in jest that if I lost my life today, that you were going home and marry Lucy. You have been my best friend, you are a noble and good man, and I now ask you in earnest to do as you said you would in jest, go back home after the war is over, marry my wife, and take care of her and my five little children."*

A year after this battle Harry and Lucy were married. They later moved to Warren County, Georgia, where they lived, died, and were buried. Lucy was the mother of fourteen children, five by her first marriage and nine by her second.

Source: 1. *Revolutionary Reader, Reminiscences and Indian Legends* by Sophie Lee Foster, pages 136-138.

Some People Take Politics Too Serious

Tory Thomas "Burnfoot" Brown denounced the patriots as savages, and he refused to sign a revolutionary petition in Georgia. A mob of patriots knocked him down, scalped him, tarred his legs and held them over a fire, and this caused two toes to burn off. He soon promised to support the American cause and was released. He immediately left town and joined with British General Robert Cunningham, and they planned the capture of Augusta for the Crown.

James W. Rabb, *Spain, British, and the American Revolution in Florida, 1763-1783,* page 84-85.

Above and Beyond

Everyone has heard of medals such as the Purple Heart, Medal of Honor, and so on. But very few have ever heard of the Badge of Military Merit, which is considered to be the first military award of the United States Armed Forces. This badge was awarded to only three soldiers.

The Continental Congress forbid General Washington from granting commissions and promotions in rank to recognize merit. Washington wanted to honor merit, especially among enlisted soldiers, so he established the Badge of Military Merit on August 7, 1782. This badge was given to the following three men along with a brace of silver-mounted pistols.

On May 3, 1783 it was presented to William Brown of the 5th Connecticut Regiment. No record of his citation exists, but it is believed that he was given the badge because of his bravery on the assault of redoubt No. 10 at Yorktown.

Also, on May 3rd Sergeant Elijah Churchill of the 2nd Regiment Light Dragoons was presented the badge. He was cited for bravery at Fort George, Tarrytown, New York, and Fort Slongo.

On June 10, 1783 Sergeant Daniel Bissell of the 2nd Connecticut Regiment was given the badge for a very unusual assignment. Under the orders of General Washington, Bissell went to New York posing as a deserter from August 14, 1781 until September 29, 1782. He joined the British army for thirteen months in the infantry, and was led by the traitor Benedict Arnold. While in the army he memorized all the information he could about the British and later returned to American lines.

After the war, the Badge of Merit was not given again, but it was never officially abolished. In 1932 it was determined that the Purple Heart Medal would be the official successor to the Badge of Military Merit.

Sources: 1. *Sergeant Elijah Churchill of the Second Continental Light Dragoons* by Donald N. Moran, Sons of Liberty Chapter, Sons of the American Revolution. 2. *Remarkable Sergeants: Ten Vignettes of Noteworthy NCOs* by CSM Dan Elder. 3. The 225th Anniversary of the Purple Heart, West Point Association of Graduates, Retrieved October 15, 2009.

How a Teeth Cleaning Helped to Lead to the Surrender of Cornwallis

All school children learn that George Washington had wooden false teeth that were made by Paul Revere. Both statements are false. What were they made of, who made them, and why did he need false teeth?

His tooth loss may have been due to his treatment for smallpox. Washington developed smallpox in 1751 while visiting Barbados. He was only nineteen and was ill for a month, and it left him with slight scarring. The positive side of the illness is that it left him immune from any further attacks. Standard treatment for smallpox was the use of a substance called mercurous chloride, which often led to the destruction of teeth.

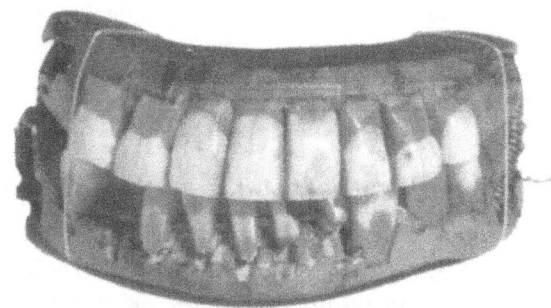

George Washington's dentures courtesy of the Mount Vernon Ladie's Association.

Examination of dental relics that have been claimed belonging to Washington determined that there were five types of teeth and tusks used to make his false teeth. The teeth were carved by hand and held in place in the mouth by using springs. Including Washington's own teeth, there were teeth made of other humans, elephants, hippos, cattle, and maybe walrus.

Washington first began having serious problems with his teeth in 1772. He sought help from a dentist by the name of John Baker. The doctor pulled several of Washington's teeth, which relieved him of immense pain. He also showed Washington, but too late, the benefits of using a toothbrush. Over the next few years he had more teeth removed. By the time he became President he had only one natural tooth remaining.

On May 29, 1781 Washington wrote a letter to Dr. Baker requesting cleaning utensils for his false teeth, *"Sir, A day or two ago I requested Col. Harrison to apply to you for a pair of Pincers to fasten the wire of my teeth. I hope you furnished him with them. I now wish you would send me one of your scrapers as my teeth stand in need of cleaning, and I have little prospect of being in Philadelph. Soon. It will come very safe by the Post and in return, the money shall be sent so soon as I know the cost of it. I am sir, Y Very H serv, G. Washington."*

Unfortunately, the letter was captured and never reached Dr. Baker. Washington was upset that the letter fell into British hands, because he liked to keep it secret about his teeth problems. Washington stated in the letter that he did not plan to be in Philadelphia anytime soon. This simple sentence convinced British General Clinton that Washington's troops, as well as the French troops camped around New York City, would not be moving south to threaten the army of General

Cornwallis at Yorktown. What Clinton did not know was that Washington was going to march to Yorktown. Once at Yorktown Cornwallis surrendered the British in October of 1781.

In 1783 Washington again needed treatment for *"some teeth which are very troublesome to me at times, and of which I wish to be eased."* This time he sought help from a French dentist, Jean-Pierre Le Mayeur. His new dentist removed some more teeth, and Washington was so pleased with his work that he invited him to his home in Virginia. The doctor visited numerous times, and he and Washington became the best of friends.

By the time Washington was President, the one remaining tooth provided the anchor for the set of hippo-tusk dentures made by dental surgeon John Greenwood. The ill-fitting dentures had a negative impact on his facial features in his later years. The dentures caused his upper and lower lips to bulge out. This resulted in the President not wanting to speak in public. Martha Washington also had problems with her dentures, which resulted in her urging her children and grandchildren to take care of their teeth.

Sources: 1. Spy letters of the American Revolution from the Collection of the Clements Library. 2. *George Washington Frontier Colonel* by Sterling North, page 29. 3. *George Washington A Biographical Companion* by Frank E. Grizzard, Jr. pages 103-104.

I Always Eat a Paper Snack When I Go For a Ride

In the summer of 1781 in South Carolina General Greene called for a volunteer messenger to carry a letter to General Sumter, but because the area was swarming with Tories no one volunteered. *"May I carry the letter,"* said sixteen year old Emily Geiger. *"They won't hurt a young girl. I am sure, and I know the way,"* she added. General Greene had no choice, so he gave the letter to the young girl and also suggested she memorize it in case she was captured. Emily mounted her horse and off she rode sidesaddle.

On the second day of her ride she encountered three Tory scouts who stopped her and took her prisoner. She was taken to the Tory commander, Lord Rawdon, who in turn took her with her guards to a Tory home several miles away. In the home was Mrs. Buxton and her daughter, and both pretended to be Tory sympathizers because the area was thick with the cruel Tories.

Many years later in 1849 Mrs. Buxton's daughter recalled her meeting with Emily Geiger. *"I went with mother,"* she said, *"to see a woman prisoner. The door of the house was guarded by the younger scout, who was Peter Simons, son of a neighbor two miles away, and a right gallant young fellow he was. After the war he married my sister. I saw the young girl and I helped mother search her. We were amazed when we saw, instead of a brazen-faced, middle-aged woman, as we supposed a spy must be, a sweet young girl about my own age, looking as innocent as a pigeon. Our sympathies were with her, but mother performed her duty faithfully. We found nothing on her person that would afford a suspicion that she was a spy."*

They found no message, because when Emily was first brought into the house she was left alone by her guard for a few minutes. This was just enough time for her to tear up the General's letter and eat it piece by piece. Emily was thankful that before she had started the ride she memorized the letter in the event she was captured.

The scouts had no choice but to release the young girl. Mrs. Buxton gave Emily some refreshments and encouraged the young girl to stay on until morning. Emily politely refused saying that because the two armies were in the area, and she should ride on to her friend's house while it was still safe. Her guard Peter Simons, who was probably smitten with Emily's beauty, offered to escort Emily to her friend's house. Again, she politely declined the invitation and rode off.

She later reached the camp of General Sumter and delivered the message almost word for word. Her ride had lasted three days and had taken her through swamps and forest. She took very little time to rest. General Sumter immediately marched his men to join with General Greene, and once they joined forces Lord Rowdon was compelled to retreat.

After Emily had returned to her home, General Greene presented her with a pair of earrings and a breastpin. Years after the war ended, General Lafayette visited the United States and presented Emily with a silk shawl. A grand ball was given in Lafayette's honor in Charlestown and Emily was present, and they danced the first minuet together.

Many years after Emily's ride, she visited the house in which she was searched. She thanked Mrs. Buxton for her kindness on that memorable day. Also, present was Mrs. Buxton's daughter who had married Emily's captor, Peter Simons. Emily and Peter compared stories of that long-ago day. Emily remarked that he was foolish to leave her unguarded for those few minutes which gave her time to eat the message. Years later Peter Simons's son and Emily Geiger's daughter married.

Sources: 1. *Women of the American Revolution* by Elizabeth Ellet, 1848. 2. *The Percy Anecdotes* by Thomas Byerly and Joseph Clinton Robertson, Vol. 2, page 155, 1834. 3. *Women Patriots of the American Revolution: a Biographical Dictionary* by Charles E. Claghorn. 4. *Five Hundred Plus Revolutionary War Obituaries and Death Notices* by Mary Harrell-Sesniak.

We Were Attacked by the Whole American Army

The Battle of Tory Hole was fought on August 27, 1781 between the patriot militia of Bladen County and the Tory militia of Bladen County. The patriots were not sure of how many of the enemy they faced so Sally Salter, the young wife of a local man, offered to enter the enemy's camp and find out.

She took a basket of eggs and took the ferry across Cape Fear River and entered the camp of the Tories. She walked around the camp selling her eggs and making mental notes of what she saw. After acquiring what she needed, she went back across the river to report her findings.

That night, because the Tories had taken all the boats, the patriots crossed the river naked with their clothes tied in bundles on top of their heads. Once across they got dressed and at daybreak took the Tory camp by surprise. The outnumbered patriots began to shout out commands to fictitious units, and many of the men also yelled out "Washington". The Tories thinking they were under attack by a large force panicked and ran. Many of the enemy ran into a deep ravine where they were easy to shoot at. This site became known as Tory Hole. Nineteen of the enemy were killed with no loss of patriot lives. Some Tory survivors of the battle reported that they were attacked by Washington's whole army.

Sources: 1. *Dictionary of North Carolina Biography: Vol. 5, P-S,* edited by William S. Powell. 2. *Historical Sketches of North Carolina from 1584 to 1851* by John H. Wheeler.

I Would Have Been Happier with a Hip, Hip, Hooray

Colonel Daniel Smith served in the Virginia Militia in the Revolutionary War. In September of 1781 he left for Yorktown, where his four sons were serving. After the American victory at Yorktown, the troops from his county of Rockingham were summoned for a review in front of the Colonel to celebrate their victory. As Colonel Smith rode by the men began firing their guns in celebration. The loud noise frighten his horse, and Colonel Smith was thrown to the ground. He died several days later from injuries received in the fall.

Sources: 1. D.A.R. Lineage Book, Vol. 10, page 315. 2. *Gleanings of Virginia History* by William Fletcher Boogher, 1903.

I've Left You Dinner, Try Not to Burn the House Down

In 1781, the British invaded New London, Connecticut and burned much of the town. During the chaos of that day an interesting story took place. The lady of one house, like other American women during the war, had her family on opposite sides of the battle. Her husband was a sergeant in the militia defending the town. Her brother was an officer under the command of General Arnold, who was invading the town. Before she fled from her home, she had her table spread and furnished with provisions. Although she was leaving with her husband, she wanted to leave a dinner for her Tory brother. As the British entered the town, her brother sought out her home, and he and several of his men ate the meal the woman left behind. The brother, at the closing of the war and in poor health, returned to the home and later died there.

Source: 1. Francis Manwaring Caulkins, *History of New London, Connecticut from the First Survey of the Coast in 1612 to 1800,* page 550.

Two of My Nine Lives Used Up in One Day

In the heat of battle during the invasion of New London, John Daboll, and a British soldier singled each other out as opponents. Both men fired at each other eight times. The eighth shot from the British soldier broke the lock of Daboll's musket and severely wounded him in the head, which ended the contest.

As John was lying there half senseless, a soldier approached him threatening to run him through with his bayonet. A British officer, who John described as "The handsomest man I ever saw," hearing John beg for his life knocked the gun to one side and said, "There you damn rebel, I have saved your life." John thanked his savior several times for saving his life. Later John was paroled and joined his wife waiting on the road for news of the battle.

Sources: 1. Local writers, *Historic Groton Comprising Historic and Descriptive Sketches,* page 50. 2. William Harris, *The Battle of Groton Heights: a Collection of Narratives, Official Reports, Records, etc. of the Storming of Fort Griswold.* This incident was related to Mr. Harris by an old man that lived in Groton, and had heard the story from John Daboll.

A Record I Would Rather Not Have

The Battle of Fort Griswold was fought on September 6, 1781 between a small Connecticut militia force and British regulars under Brigadier General Benedict Arnold. The American commander Colonel William Ledyard handed over his sword as a sign of surrender to a British officer. The officer took the sword and killed Colonel Ledyard with it. Lambert Latham, a slave that belonged to American Captain William Latham, took a bayonet and killed the British officer. Other British soldiers swarmed over Lambert and killed him. The slave was stabbed thirty-three times, which was probably the most bayonet wounds received by anyone in the Revolution.

Source: 1. *The Untold Story of the Black Regiment: Fighting in the Revolutionary War* by Michael Burgan.

Don't Mess with My Mama

Fort Griswold was captured on September 6, 1781 by the British led by the American traitor Benedict Arnold. Captain William Latham was wounded in the thigh and taken along with his ten year old son William and other prisoners under guard.

As the town of New London was being looted and burned by the British, the wife of Captain Latham and her daughter Mary made their way to the fort to look for her husband and son. She first went to Ebenezer Avery's house, which was being used as a hospital. At the door the sentry held out his rifle to prevent them from entering. Unafraid, Mrs. Latham pushed his rifle aside and went into the house. Once inside she saw wounded friends and neighbors but did not find her family. She kept looking all night, and in the morning she went to the headquarters' of Arnold and asked about her son.

She found young William sitting with the other prisoners paralyzed with terror and in great distress. It was the 7th of September and the boy had no food since the night of the 5th. He was fatigued from the heat and the fear of all he had seen in the battle. He had a piece of bread in his hand but had not eaten it for fear that the British had poisoned it.

Mrs. Latham knew Benedict Arnold well since he was a native of Norwich. She said to him, *"Benedict Arnold, I come for my child. Not to ask for him but demand him of you."* *"Take him,"* replied Arnold. *"Take him, and don't you bring him up a damned rebel."* *"I shall take him,"* she said, *"and teach him to despise the name of a traitor."* All members of the Latham family survived the war.

Sources: 1. *Genealogical Notes of the Williams and Gallup Families* by Charles F. Williams, 1897. 3. *The Connecticut Magazine, Vol. 9* by William Farrand Felch, George Atwell, H. Phelps Arms, and Francis Treelyan Miller, 1905.

Sorry, We Are on Our Break Now

The Battle of Eutaw Springs was fought on September 8, 1781 in South Carolina. The hot day began with the Americans, short on rest and food, advancing toward the springs. The Americans forced the British from their camp leaving their uneaten breakfast. The American troops stopped their advance, and they began eating the deserted breakfast and plundering the stores of food and liquor. They ignored the officer's commands to continue the fight. Soon the British regrouped and launched a counter attack and they forced the Americans out of the camp. The battle ended in a draw with both sides claiming a victory. If the Americans had not stopped to eat and drink while chasing the British, it might have been an American victory.

Sources: 1. *Teetotalers and Saloon Smashers: The Temperance Movement and Prohibition* by Richard Worth. 2. *A Guide to the Battles of the American Revolution* by Theodore P. Savas and J. David Dameron. 3. *Holden's Dollar Magazine, Vol. 1, Number 1, January 1, 1848*.

Couldn't We Just Stand in the Trench and Stick Out Our Tongues at Them?

During the siege of Yorktown in October of 1781, the Americans began to dig trenches to encircle the British forces. After the trenches were ready American troops were sent in to occupy them. The British began firing some of their cannons at the Americans as Colonel Alexander Hamilton took his men to the trench. Hamilton had his troops stand along the top of the trench and face the British lines, which were about 600 yards away. He ordered the men to go through the manual of arms in clear view of the British cannons. He wanted to impress upon the British that his men had no fear of British cannons. The British soldiers looking on in amazement held their fire.

One of Hamilton's men, Captain James Duncan, wrote about it in his journal, *"We were ordered to mount the bank, front the enemy, and there by word of command go through all the ceremony of soldiery, ordering and grounding our arms; and although the enemy had been firing a little before, they did not give us a single shot. I suppose their astonishment at our conduct must have prevented them, for I can assign no other reason. Colonel Hamilton gave the orders, and although I esteem him one of the first officers in the American army, must beg leave in this instance to think he wantonly exposed the lives of his men."*

Source: Egle, William Henry, *Journals and Diaries of the War of the Revolution with Lists of Officers and Soldiers, 1775-1783, Journal of Captain James Duncan.* Harrisburg, PA, 1893, page 749.

General Humor

During the early days of the Siege of Yorktown the Americans and French engaged in digging trenches at night. One finished they would place cannons and fire on the encircled British. While the digging was going on during the night General von Steuben was there with General Wayne. A shell fired by the British landed near the two men. The Baron threw himself into the trench and Wayne followed falling on top of him. .The Baron seeing that it was Wayne on top of him, said *"I always knew you were brave, general, but I did not know that you were so perfect in every point of duty; you cover your general's retreat in the best manner possible."*

Source: *The Life of Frederick William Von Steuben Major General in the Revolutionary Army* by Frederick Kapp. Page 457.

Humor in War

Lieutenant Edward Manning was leading his American Company at the Battle of Eutaw Springs on September 8, 1781. When the British 3rd Regiment of Foot broke and ran, they were pursued by Manning's Company. Manning was leading the charge, and in his excitement he did not notice that he had outrun his men.

He soon found himself surrounded by British troops and no Americans in sight. Something had to be done, so Manning grabbed a British officer standing near him. He took the sword from the Englishman and used him for a shield. The shocked Englishman did not try to escape, instead he began to give Manning his various titles. *"I am sir, Sir Henry Barry, Deputy Adjutant General of the British Army, Captain of the 52nd Regiment, Secretary to the Commandant of Charleston."*

Manning who was not impressed said, *"Enough, you are just the man I have been looking for. Fear nothing; you shall screen me from danger and I will take special care of you."* Manning held the surprised man in front of him, until he reached the American line and handed his prisoner over.

Sources: 1. *Revolutionary Reader, Reminiscences and Indian Legends* by Sophie Lee Foster, page, 188. 2. *Eutaw Springs: The Final Battle of the American Revolution's Southern Campaign* by Robert M. Dunkerly and Irene B. Boland.

***

During the Siege of Augusta in May of 1781 two men were arrested for a crime and condemned to die. An executioner could not be found, and no soldier in the army wanted the job. It was finally decided that the least guilty of the pair would be set free, on the condition that he serve as the hangman for the other man.

The terms of the condition were accepted, and the man who was to be set free had little time to celebrate his change of luck. Right after the released man had hung his companion, a four pound shot from the British struck him in the chest and killed him. The unlucky man dropped dead at the side of the man he had just hung.

Source: 1. *Anecdotes of the Revolutionary War in America: with Sketches of Character* by Alexander Garden, page 405.

***

Colonel Peter Horry of the South Carolina Militia was afflicted by a speech impediment that nearly caused him to lose his life and the lives of his men. He was ordered to wait and ambush a British detachment that was approaching. As the enemy approached he could not get the words to come out of his mouth. All that would come out was, *"Fi, fi, fi."* As the British grew near he finally shouted, *"Shoot damn you, shoot. You know very well what I would say."*

Another time during battle a fellow officer said to him, *"I am wounded Colonel."* Horry hollered back to the man, *"Think no more of it, Baxter, but stand your post."* Soon the man called out again, *"But I can't, Colonel, I am wounded a second time."* Horry replied, *"Then lie down, Baxter, but quit not your post."* A third time the wounded man yelled out, *"Colonel, they have shot me again, and if I remain longer here I shall be shot to pieces."* *"Be it so, Baxter,"* replied Horry, *"but stir not."*

Source: 1. *Revolutionary Reader, Reminiscences and Indian Legends* by Sophie Lee Foster, pages, 188-189.

Time for Payback

Days after the surrender of Cornwallis the townspeople of Yorktown sought to reclaim items that the British had taken from them. Lieutenant Colonel Banastre Tarleton, the hated British officer, was publicly humiliated when a man named Mr. Day threatened the Colonel with a wooden stick and demanding the return of the black stallion the Colonel was riding. The Colonel gave up the animal without a fuss, which delighted the crowd of onlookers.

Sources: 1. Pension Papers R5464 of Irvine Hyde. 2. *Let the Drums Roll: Veterans and Patriots of the Revolutionary War Who Settled in Maury County, Tennessee* by Marise Parrish Lightfoot. 3. *The Guns of Independence: The Siege of Yorktown, 1781* by Jerome A. Green.

He Should Have Jumped Over the Cannonball

John Deane stated in his pension application an event that took place at Yorktown. *"I remember the cannon ball came rolling on the ground at the siege of York, there was a man present saying he would stop the ball and in attempting to do so he lost both of his legs."*

Source: 1. Pension application W699.

Do We Get Extra Credit?

In 1781 at Yorktown Joseph Cabell commanded a Buckingham Regiment of militia that had a company made of students, including his son from William and Mary College.

Sources: 1. *So Obscure a Person* by Edna Barney. 2. D.A.R. Lineage Book, Vol. 66, page 316.

It Pays to be Nosey

Sixteen year old Susanna Bolling was not happy when in 1781 Lord Cornwallis took over her family home to quarter his officers. One evening she happened to overhear the British officers discussing plans to attack the troops commanded by the Marquis de Lafayette. She knew where the American headquarters were located, and she decided to warn them of the upcoming attack.

In the cellar of the house there was a tunnel that had been built in case of Indian raids, and it led to the Appomattox River. Susanna went through the tunnel, and at the end was a small boat by the river. She rowed across the river to a neighboring farm house and borrowed a horse. She rode to the headquarters of Lafayette.

She was taken directly to Lafayette and told him what she had overheard at her home. Lafayette now had time to evade the British troops and to get a warning to General Washington. Soon after the British were defeated at Yorktown, and it is very possible that this young girl helped to make that victory possible with her warning.

Source: 1. *Women Patriots of the American Revolution a Biographical Dictionary* by Charles E. Claghorn.

Marquis de Lafayette.

A Storm Defeats the British Army

In school we learned that General Washington surrounded the British General Cornwallis at the Battle of Yorktown forcing the British to surrender, and as a result won our independence. What we didn't learn was that the victory was made possible by a sudden freak storm.

Across the York River from Yorktown is a point of land that juts out into the channel and narrows the river to half a mile called Gloucester. There 1,000 British troops with their backs to the river faced an equal number of French and American troops. Gloucester was the escape route from Yorktown for the British army. Cornwallis had decided to remove the majority of his troops from Yorktown and ferry them across the river at night to Gloucester. Once across the Americans and French troops would be greatly outnumbered and no match for the British. Cornwallis would then be able to escape out of Virginia with most of his army intact.

The escape was put into action on the night of October 16, 1781. British troops began to load onto boats very quietly, and the first wave of boats carried 1,000 troops across the York River. As Cornwallis was preparing to leave in the second wave, he wrote a letter to Washington requesting that the General show mercy to the small detachment of British soldiers he was leaving behind in Yorktown.

Then, a miracle occurred, at least from the patriot's point of view. Before the second wave of boats were launched, a hard storm blew in and scattered boats downstream that were caught on the river. A hard windy rain fell until two in the morning. It was now impossible to move the British troops across.

The Americans had moved their cannons closer to the British positions at Yorktown and Cornwallis had no choice but to surrender or face annihilation. On October 17, 1781 the British surrendered their army to General Washington.

Sources: 1. *The Virginia Campaign and the Blockade and Siege of Yorktown* by Army War College Historical Section, Howard Lee Landers, page 202. 2. *Battles of the American Revolution, 1775-1781* by Henry Beebee Carrington, page 640. 3. *The Guns of Independence: The Siege of Yorktown, 1781* by Jerome Greene, pages 38 & 75.

It's a Good Thing He Didn't Yell Out Stupid

One of the best and most heroic American Generals in the American Revolution was General "Mad" Anthony Wayne. You might think by the General's nickname that he was angry or a grump most of the time. Mad had nothing to do with his temper. The nickname was given to him by a character known as "Jemmy the Rover."

Jemmy was Wayne's main spy during the war, and while in Virginia just before the Siege of Yorktown Jemmy was thrown in a cell at a local jail. When Jemmy was released and when he returned to camp General Wayne was not very happy that Jemmy had not been out gathering intelligence on the British. Jemmy became angry and unruly, and the General had him arrested and sentenced to receive twenty-nine lashes.

Jemmy was really angry when he found out that his friend Wayne had ordered him to receive lashes. As Jemmy was being led away he yelled out, *"Anthony is mad. He must be mad or he would help me. Mad Anthony, that's what he is. Mad Anthony Wayne."* The event spread around the camp and since the words *"Mad Anthony Wayne"* had a rhythm and a nice cadence, the soldiers picked it up and began to use it.

Sources: 1. *Mad Anthony Wayne and the New Nation: The Story of Washington's Front-Line General* by Glenn Tucker. 2. *Anthony Wayne, Soldier of the Early Republic* by Paul David Nelson, 1985.

If that's What You Want, but I Think it is Rather Dumb

The Battle of Johnstown occurred on October 25, 1781, and during the battle there were several small skirmishes. During one of the skirmishes Joseph Wagner, one of the American militiamen, shot a British officer as the Americans retreated. After the battle, Wagner went back to the battlefield and found the wounded officer. Wagner told him, *"My dear sir, I am the man who shot you in the afternoon, but I have a fellow feeling for you. Permit me and I will take you to our camp, where you shall receive kind treatment and good care.* The officer replied, *"I would rather die on this spot, than leave it with a damed rebel!"* Wagner granted the man his request and left him to die.

Sources: 1. *The Bloodied Mohawk: The American Revolution in the Words of Fort Planks Defenders and Other Mohawk Valley Partisans* by Kenneth D. Johnson. 2. *History of Schoharie County and Border Wars of New York, Vol. 2* by Jeptha R. Simms.

I Thought They Were My Friends

John Cock was enlisted in a Virginia Regiment in the year 1777 and served for eighteen months. He also volunteered to serve in the Virginia Militia in 1781. One day he visited a friend, and the next morning barking dogs woke him. He went outside to look and came face to face with four armed Cherokee Indians. His friends inside the house saw the Indians and bolted the front door leaving John to face the hostiles alone and with no weapon.

John took off running toward the woods with two of the Indians in pursuit. After running about two hundred yards he faced the Indians and tried to surrender. He described what happens next in his pension application filed in 1834,

"Each of the merciless savages instantly drew from their belts their Tomahawks and stepped up to me. One of them immediately struck me upon my bare head for I had left my hat in the house with the pole of his Tomahawk and sunk it into my skull, and gave me a lick with the edge of the Ax, which sunk in to my head and touched my Brain. I fell lifeless and Indians no doubt believed me to be so. They immediately scalped me and pulled my hunting shirt off of me and cut one half of my waistcoat off and took them with them. In a short time I came to my senses my neck was entirely limber I had no use of my left arm or shoulder or have I ever regained the use of my shoulder or arm."

John died three months after filing his application. There is no record of the names of the "friends" that locked him out, or if they remained friends.

Source: 1. Pension file of John Cock S3171.

Aren't You a Little Old to Play Jump Rope?

Prims Hall was born to a slave on February 29, 1756 in Boston, and at the age of nineteen he enlisted in the army. In 1781 Primus became a steward to Quartermaster Colonel Thomas Pickering.

One anecdotal story about Primus and George Washington appeared in several publications in the 1800's. When Washington visited the camp of Colonel Pickering he sometimes felt the need for exercise. Primus would get a rope and fastened one end to a stake about breast high, and he would hold the other end taut at his chest several feet away. Washington then would run and jump over the rope again and again until he tired. Whenever Washington visited the camp he would say, *"Come, Primus, I am in need of exercise."*

Another story occurred late one night when Washington was at the camp of Colonel Pickering. Primus found some straw and a blanket and made Washington a bed. After the General had fallen asleep Primus sat on a box or stool and leaned his head into his hands to sleep. Primus had given the General the last of the straw and the last blanket for his bedding.

Washington awoke during the night and saw Primus asleep sitting on the stool and he realized that he had been given the last of the bedding. He woke Primus up and insisted that Primus join him in his bed since there was enough room for two people. It was not uncommon during that period for travelers to share the same bed at inns when space was limited or share on the ground during cold weather.

Sources: 1. Report of the Committee Appointed to Revise the Soldier's Record, page 153. 2. *This is New Jersey* by John T. Cunningham, page 46. 3. Pension Application W751. 4. *Encyclopedia of African-American Education* by Faustine Childness Jones-Wilson, page 200. 5. *Making Slavery History: Abolitionism and the Politics of Memory in Massachusetts* by Margot Minardi, pages 63-9. 6. *Washington: The Indispensable Man* by James Thomas Flexner, page 120.

Joining a New Family

In 1781 eighteen year old Horatio Jones joined with Captain Boyd of the United States Army in pursuit of the Indians that had raided their settlement. One morning the soldiers were trapped by the Indians in an ambush. Horatio tried to run to safety but was captured. A man called Jack Berry, half-white and half-Indian, told Horatio that he did not need to be afraid and that he would make a good Indian boy. A Seneca woman had asked Berry to find a captive to replace her son that had been killed in battle.

Horatio saw several of the American captives tortured and killed as the party made their way to the Indian village. He gained the respect of the Seneca, because Horatio showed no sign of hunger, fatigue, or anger. Once when one of the Indians killed a deer, Horatio and several other young Indians were sent to retrieve the animal. A foot race to the fallen animal began between Horatio and the fastest Indian runner named Sharp Shins. The Indian earned the name as a runner from the British at Fort Niagara. They said he ran so fast that his shins cut the air. Horatio beat Sharp Shins to the deer, and as a result he won further respect from the Indians and the hatred of Sharp Shins. Horatio now was treated a little more leniently than the other prisoners.

When the group finally reached the Indian camp at Caneadea, the captives were forced to run the gauntlet. Many Indian tribes had this ceremony for the amusement of the tribe and for the captives to atone for their people's wrongs to the Indians. Each prisoner would have to run a certain distance from the starting point to the council house. The route was between two lines of old men, squaws, and young boys armed with various weapons to strike the captives as they ran by.

Horatio was able to run the gauntlet with minimal injury thanks to what Jack Berry whispered to him. Berry told Horatio the trick was to follow very close behind the next to last runner and stay near one line of attackers. By staying near the line, it would prevent the attackers to have ample time or room to hit him. The trick was successful for Horatio. However, the man in front of him was beaten so badly that his head was nearly sliced off. Besides Horatio, Captain Boyd survived the gauntlet and was later turned over to the British.

That night at council Horatio was accepted into the Indian tribe. Jack Berry told the council that he was asked to bring a young boy back to replace the son that one of the women had lost. The woman was the sister of the Chief of the tribe, Chief Shongo. Horatio was welcomed into the tribe and was given the name Hoc-sa-go-Wah, which meant "handsome boy." His adoptive Indian mother thought he was the most handsome young man she had ever seen. In time Horatio would gain great influence over the Indians. They grew to respect his honesty, bravery, and strength.

Horatio realized that with nearly 200 miles of wilderness from home and without a compass or trail, that escape was not very possible. He accepted his situation, learned their language, and entered into the life as a tribe member. He became fluent in the language of the Seneca and served as an interpreter. He took on the job of questioning white captives, and he tried to please his Indian family and save the captives from harm.

Major Van Campen of the U.S. Army was captured by the Seneca Indians and taken back to the village for interrogation by Horatio. The Major had earlier earned a reputation as an Indian killer. In April of 1782 the Major was captured and held by a small group of Indians, and he was able to escape when he got free and killed his captives. If his new captives learned of what he had previously done, they would have quickly put him to death.

When the Indians and their captive arrived at the village, he was questioned by Horatio who knew who the Major was. The Indians asked Horatio if he knew the prisoner's name. Horatio answered truthfully, *"I have never seen him before."* Horatio knew of the Major, but this was the first time he had ever seen him. He kept the Major's secret, and the Indians later turned the Major over to the British. Horatio had saved the Major's life.

Horatio became famous throughout the region. A British officer named Captain Powell offered to buy at any price Horatio's freedom from the Seneca. The Indian chief refused saying that the boy was sent by the Great Spirit as a special gift for the good of the tribe. He ended by saying, *"A Seneca will not sell his own blood."* Horatio was later appointed as a chief with the new name of Ta-ya-da-o-who-koh meaning "lying across," symbolizing his bonding of whites with Indians.

In one of the other captive's tribe was a young white woman named Sarah Whitmore. She confided in Horatio of her concerns about an Indian she did not like wanting to marry her. Horatio solved the problem by asking her to marry him. They were married by a missionary in 1784 after being freed from the Indians by the Treaty of Stanwix.

In 1785 Horatio became a fur trader, and he built a log cabin for his family on Seneca Lake. One evening a young man came to his door. He had just started a career as a trapper and was now lost. He purchased the entire stock of Horatio's furs and hired him to collect pelts exclusively for him and to deliver them to New York City. This partnership between Horatio Jones and John Jacob Astor continued for many years.

When Sarah died in 1792, Horatio married seventeen year old Elizabeth Starr in 1793. They were given a 3,000 acre farm by the Indians. The Indians feared the area was haunted by a headless ghost, but they thought Horatio's powers would be able to counteract its evil.

In his later years he became a prosperous farmer and kept contact with many of his old friends. At one dinner, given in his honor, several Indian chiefs were invited including his old rival Sharp Shins. The two old men smoked a peace pipe to put an end to their rivalry.

Sources: 1. *History of Livingston County, New York 1678-1881* by Doty Smith, 1876. 2. *Sketches of Border Adventures in the Life of Major Moses Van Campen* by John Hubbard, 1842. 3. *The Divided Ground-Indians, Settlers, & Northern Borderland of the American Revolution* by Alan Taylor. 4. *Ghosts & Hauntings of the Finger Lakes* by Patti Unvericht. 5. Lineage Book D.A.R. Vol. 39, 1906. 6. Sons of the American Revolution Application. 7. Tombstone. 8. Pension Papers S23728.

No Friend of the British

Andrew Jackson's father died shortly before Andrew was born on March 15, 1767 in Waxhaws, which was on the border of North and South Carolina. Andrew always claimed South Carolina as his birth state. Andrew's mother hoped he would become a Presbyterian minister, but she saw that there was little chance for that to happen. Young Andrew enjoyed playing pranks, cursing, and fighting, which was hardly the proper background for becoming a minister.

When Andrew was thirteen his brother Hugh got his mother's permission to join the American army. At the Battle of Stono fought on June 20, 1779 Hugh was ill and told not to engage in the battle, however, he joined in the battle. He died after the battle from heat exhaustion and fatigue.

In 1781 Andrew was fourteen when he first took part in the revolution. *"I was never regularly enlisted, being only fourteen when the war practically ended. Whenever I took the field it was with Colonel Davie, who never put me in the ranks, but used me as a mounted orderly or messenger for which I was well fitted, being a good rider and knowing all the roads in that region. The only weapons I had were a pistol that Colonel Davie gave me and a small fowling-piece that my Uncle Crawford lent me."*

"I was in one skirmish, that of Sands House, and there they caught me, along with my brother Robert and my cousin Tom Crawford."

Andrew and Robert were now prisoners of the hated British dragoons. During their captivity one of the officers approached Andrew and ordered the young boy to clean off his boots. Andrew, who was noted for his temper replied, *"Sir, I am a prisoner of war and claim to be treated as such."*

The officer became enraged that a young boy, and a despicable rebel besides that, would address him in such a manner. The officer drew his saber and swung it at Andrew who ducked and at the same time raised his left hand to block the blow. The saber cut Andrew's head and gashed his fingers. Andrew would carry the scars from this encounter for the rest of his life. As an adult he would sometimes run his fingers over the scar on his head as a reminder for his hatred for the British. The officer then shipped Andrew and Robert off to a prison at Camden, South Carolina.

British prisons were noted for their harsh conditions and treatment. Their prisons had no bedding, medicine, and little food. Soon both boys contracted the dreaded smallpox. Their mother was determined to get the boys released to save them. Some accounts suggest that she arranged a prisoner exchange of British soldiers for her boys and several other Americans. Another account reports that an exchange was taking place at the time, and she persuaded the British to include her two sons in the exchange. Whatever happened she managed the release of her boys and faced a long journey home with only two horses to carry the three of them.

Poor Robert was so sick that he could not sit upright and had to be lashed to the horse. She rode the other horse, and Andrew walked along side with bare feet. Just before they reached home there was a hard rain that soaked the weary travelers. Two days later Robert died, and Andrew was down with the pox and a fever. When Andrew finally recovered he said, *"When it left me, I was a skeleton, not quite six feet long and a little over six inches thick! It took me all the rest of that year (1781) to recover my strength and get flesh enough to hide my bones."* By the time he recovered Cornwallis had surrendered and the war was almost over in the south.

Andrew's mother went to Charleston Harbor to care for her cousins who were among the sick and wounded Americans in British prison ships. While there she caught cholera and died. When the war had finally ended in September of 1783, Andrew had lost his father, mother, and both brothers during the war. He blamed the British for his loses. Andrew probably never imagined that he would grow up to become the 7th President of the United States.

Sources: 1. *Best Little Stories from the American Revolution* by C. Brian Kelly. 2. *A History of Andrew Jackson* by Augustus C. Buell, 1904. 3. *Life of Andrew Jackson* by Marquis James, 1938. 4. *Young Andrew Jackson in the Carolinas: A Revolutionary Boy* by Jennifer Hunsicker.

Never Question Daniel Boone

The Battle of Blue Licks was fought on August 18, 1782. A group of about 50 Loyalists and 300 Indians raided into Kentucky and began to leave after two days. A force of Kentucky militiamen began to pursue them. As the Kentuckians got close, Daniel Boone, a leader and very skilled woodsman, suspected a trap and wanted to wait for reinforcements. Another leader, Hugh McGary, wanted to prove he was no coward and he decided to attack at once. He mounted his horse and yelled out, *"Them that ain't cowards, follow me."* As the men began to attack Boone replied, *"We are all slaughtered men."*

As Boone had feared they rode into a trap. Many Indians were concealed in the bushy ravine and almost surrounded the Kentucky militiamen. They tried to retreat back down the hill and had to fight hand-to-hand with the Indians behind them. Boone grabbed a horse and told his twenty-three year old son Israel to get on it. As soon as Israel mounted the horse, he fell to the ground, shot dead with a bullet wound to the neck. Daniel then grabbed the horse and retreated. He later retrieved his son's body and brought it back to the fort.

Many of the mounted men escaped, while most of the men on foot were slaughtered. Of the 180 Kentucky militiamen seventy-two were killed, including Captain Joseph Kincaid. Years later whenever Daniel Boone spoke of the defeat, he would be overcome with grief and openly cry.

Sources: 1. *The Encyclopedia of Northern Kentucky* edited by Paul A. Tenkotte, James C. Claypool. 4. *The Pictorial Field-Book of the Revolution Vol I* by Benson John Lossing. 5. Pension Papers S16907.

Feet, Don't Desert Me Now

Elizabeth Zane and her family moved into the area that is now Wheeling, West Virginia. The family and several others established Fort Henry in this wilderness. It was surrounded by thick woods, and the Indians in the area were very much pro-British. On September 11, 1782 Fort Henry was attacked by British and their Indian allies.

The fort had only about sixteen fighting men and the rest were women and children. During the attack Elizabeth, age sixteen, occupied the sentry box with her brother Jonathan and John

Saltar. Her job was to load the guns for the two men. The people inside the fort were facing over 300 enemy fighters. The supply of powder soon dwindled to just a few loads left.

Elizabeth's brother Ebenezer remembered that he had carelessly left a keg of gunpowder back at their home, which was about sixty yards from the fort's gate. Colonel Zane, Elizabeth's father, called the men together and said that someone who was a fast runner would need to go for the powder. He reminded them of the danger of the journey, and he said there would be a good chance the runner would be shot down by the enemy.

Several of the boys volunteered. However, the Colonel was hesitant to let them leave. They could not afford to lose any of the fighting men, and Elizabeth knowing this volunteered. She told her father she was aware of the danger but should she fall her loss would be less important than if a fighting man was to fall. She told her father, *"You have not one man to spare; a woman will not be missed in the defense of the fort."*

The men opened the gate, and Elizabeth stepped outside and began walking at a fast pace. The Indians looked at her and did not consider her any threat, several of them yelled, *"Squaw, Squaw"* as she passed by. She quickly made it to the house, and she tied a tablecloth around her waist and poured the powder in it. As she started back to Fort Henry, the enemy realized what this girl was up to and began firing at her. Ball after ball whizzed past her as she ran back to the fort. She entered the fort unharmed with only one musket ball hole in her dress. About two days later a relief force was sent, and the Indians and British retreated. Her feat is even more impressive, because she had gone without sleep for the past forty hours. Her bravery is immortalized in a book written in 1903 by her descendant, Zane Grey, entitled *Betty Zane*.

Lithograph by Nagel and Weingaertner from Library of Congress. "Heroism of Miss Elizabeth Zane."

Sources: 1. *Young and Brave: Girls Changing History*. 2. *The Women of the American Revolution, Vol. 2* by Elizabeth Fries Ellet. 3. Elizabeth Zane Chapter, West Virginia State Society, D.A.R. 3. *Some Pennsylvania Women during the War of the Revolution* edited by William Henry Egle.

Life Guards That Never Went Into the Water

In 1776 a unit was formed known as Washington's Life Guard with the job of protecting the General. The guard was with him in all of his battles and was disbanded in 1783. The number of guards varied from 180 to 250 and care was given to select men from every colony.

The men selected for this prestigious duty had to meet strict standards. They had to be good men that were recommended for their sobriety, honesty, and good behavior. They had to stand between five feet eight inches to five feet ten inches tall. They should be handsome and well made, clean, and neat. Cleanliness was very important to Washington, and he encouraged all the troops under him to try to remain clean. He also wanted men born in America, but he did not want the men aware that this was a requirement because he did not want to *"create any invidious distinction between them and the foreigners."*

Sources: 1. *The Commander in Chief's Guard, Revolutionary War* by Carlos Emmor Godfrey. 2. D.R.A. Lineage Book, Vol. 7, page 33.

I Think I'll Sit the War Out

Stephen McGown may have the honor of being a prisoner for the longest continual period of time in the Revolutionary War. He was taken prisoner by Indians and held for five years. At the age of fifteen Stephen served as a private in the 6th New York Infantry of Colonel Alden's Regiment. When the British and Indians overran Cherry Valley in November of 1778, Stephen was shot in the wrist just before he was taken prisoner by the Indians.

He was spared probably because of his young age, and he was then forced to march to Fort Niagara with a group of women and children. When he reached Fort Niagara, he was taken sick and confined in the hospital. When he recovered he was purchased from the Indians by Captain Powell of the British Army.

Stephen was then taken to Castle Island, then to Oswego, and finally to Kingston in Canada where he remained as a servant to the Captain until 1783. When the treaty to end the Revolutionary War was signed he was permitted to return home to Cherry Valley. Stephen walked over 140 miles to return home. For his service in the war he received a yearly pension of $80.

Sources: 1. Pension Application of Stephen McGown. 2. D.A.R. Lineage Book, Vol. 6, page 126. 3. U.S. Pension Roll of 1835.

Ben Franklin Gets the Last Word

Many years after the victory of George Washington, with the aid of the French over the British, a dinner with diplomats was given. Attending were the French and English Ambassadors along with Benjamin Franklin of the United States. The English Ambassador rose and gave a toast to his homeland, *"To England, the sun whose bright beams enlighten and fructify the remotest corners of the earth."*

Not to be outdone, the French Ambassador rose and politely said, *"To France, the moon whose mild steady, and cheering rays are the delight of all nations, consoling them in darkness and making their dreariness beautiful."*

Ben Franklin slowly rose and in a very dignified way he said, *"To George Washington, the Joshua who commanded the sun and the moon to stand still, and they obeyed him."*

Source: 1. *Revolutionary Reader, Reminiscences and Indian Legends* by Sophie Lee Foster, page, 139.

National Archives

Chapter 7

"I dare say the men would fight very well if properly officered, although they are an exceedingly dirty and nasty people." George Washington about his own army.

Strange Events

Two for One

Jim Capers, described as a free man of color, filed for a Revolutionary War pension in 1849 at the age of 107. When asked why he waited so long to file, he said that he did not know a free man of color was entitled to receive a pension. His application contained an unusual event.

According to his pension Jim served for more than seven years and was engaged in several battles. At the Battle of Eutaw Springs, often described as the bloodiest of the battles during the war, he received two saber cuts to the head and one to his face. The strangest wound was when a shot passed through his side and killed the drummer, Paul Ram Lee, standing behind him.

"That in the last mentioned Battle, affiant was wounded, in four Different places, one on the head & two on the face with a sword and one on the left side with a ball. Killing the drummer Immediately behind him, whose name was Paul Ram Lee." Statement taken from Jim's pension application.

Source: 1. Pension Application of Jim Capers R1669.

I Volunteered to Do What?

During the Revolutionary War, slave owners or another family member would get drafted into the service, so they would send their slaves to serve in their place. Tim Jones was the slave of a Virginia farmer by the name of Rolling Jones. Rolling did not get drafted, but he did go out drinking one day. While he was drunk, he enlisted during the latter part of the war in a Virginia Regiment.

When Rolling Jones sobered up he realized he had made a terrible mistake. So he did the only honorable thing; which was to send his slave Tim Jones to serve in his place. Tim served with honor for the next year, and although he lost his leg at the Battle of Yorktown he gained his freedom when he was discharged.

Source: 1. Pension Application S18063 for Tim Jones.

Mamma Always Said I Was Hard Headed

Doctor James Thacher served for eight years in the Revolutionary War. In the diary he kept he wrote about a very lucky soldier. *"A brave soldier received a musket ball in his forehead, observing that it did not penetrate deep, it was imagined that the ball rebounded and fell out; but after several days, on examination, I detected the ball laying flat on the bone, and spread under the skin, which I removed. No one can doubt but he received his wound while facing the enemy, and it is fortunate for the brave fellow, that his skull proved too thick for the ball to penetrate."*

Source: 1. Military Journal during the American Revolution from 1775 to 1783 by Dr. James Thacher, 1823.

We Owe it All to Eating a Carrot a Day

During the Revolutionary War the Pennsylvania 1st Regiment, also known as the Pennsylvania, had quite the reputation as marksmen. Doctor James Thacher describes them in his diary: *"They are remarkably stout and hardy men; many of them exceeding six feet in height. They are dressed in white frocks or rifle shirts and round hats. There are men remarkable for the accuracy of their aim; striking a mark with great certainty at two hundred yards distance. At a review, a company of them, while in a quick advance, fired balls into objects of seven inches diameter at the distance of 250 yards...their shot have frequently proved fatal to British officers and soldiers who expose themselves to view at more than double the distance of common musket shot."*

Source: 1. *Military Journal during the American Revolutionary War 1775 to 1783* by Dr. James Thacher, 1834.

We Can Still Do the Job

One of the most unusual regiments in the Revolutionary War was the Invalid Regiment. It was composed of Continental Army veterans who had become unfit for field duty but still wanted to serve in some capacity. In 1777 Lewis Nicola proposed to the Continental Congress the formation of the Invalid Regiment.

Congress accepted his recommendation and placed Nicola in charge. About 1,000 troops were divided into eight companies of soldiers and they were stationed at various places in Pennsylvania. Their duty was to serve as guards for magazines, hospitals, and installations that were similar. The regiment was transferred to West Point and was disbanded at the end of the war.

Sources: 1. *The Nicola Affair: Lewis Nicola, George Washington, and American Military Discontent during the Revolutionary War* by Robert F. Haggard. 2. *Encyclopedia of Continental Army Units: Battalions, Regiments, and Independent Corps.* by Fred Anderson Berg. 3. D.A.R. Lineage Book, Vol. 4, page 83.

You Look Taller in Person

Zephon Flower, age fourteen, was on guard duty one night when he was approached by General George Washington. Young Zephon halted the General and requested the countersign. Washington stopped, gave the countersign, they saluted, and as Washington left he tossed the boy a half dollar saying, *"Good boy, good soldier."*

Sources: 1. *A History of Old Tioga Point and Early Athens, Pennsylvania,* by Louise Welles Murray. 2. *History of Bradford County, Pennsylvania.* 3. Pension Papers S6856. 4. Sons of the American Revolution Application. 5. *Historical Register of the Colorado Society of the Sons of the American Revolution, November 1, 1905 to February 1, 1912.*

The First Stealth Wagon

John Goodard was a wagon master general during the period the British occupied Boston. He worked in darkness and by stealth constructing American fortifications on Dorchester Heights, which overlooked Boston. It was important that the Americans get weapons and ammunitions to the patriots inside of Boston.

John had an ingenious plan to sneak a wagon load of supplies inside Boston. John got one of wagons and loaded it with arms and ammunition and then piled lumber over the cargo. He disguised himself as a teamster, and covered the oxen's feet with carpet to reduce any noise. His plan worked, and he succeeded in getting the supplies to the patriots.

Sources: 1. *Burials and Inscriptions in the Walnut Street Cemetery* by Alma Cummings, 1920. 2. D.A.R. Lineage Book, Vol. 3, page 122.

All in a Day's Work

Samuel Frazee was an Indian fighter and a soldier serving under Colonel Joseph Bowman. He purchased his land in Kentucky from the Indians for several hundred bushels of salt. One day he was plowing in his field and noticed three Indians creeping through the corn toward his house where his family was. Without stopping his ox team, he silently climbed a nearby maple tree and shot the three warriors. He climbed down the tree and continued his plowing.

Sources: 1. D.A.R. Lineage Book, Vol. 6, page 243. 2. *The WPA Guide to Kentucky the Bluegrass State* by Federal Writer's Project.

British Justice

George Washington spent many nights at the home of Martha and John Van Doren in New Jersey. Knowing this the British visited their home one day and took the couple prisoner and demanded information about the patriot army. Martha refused to give any information, so the British hung her by her heels to force her to talk. She still refused and when her faced started to turn black they released her.

Sources: 1. Sons of the American Revolution Application. 2. D.A.R. Lineage Book, Vol. 146, page 281.

Maybe I Should Go on a Diet

As the war progressed Colonel Israel Shreve's weight had ballooned up to 320 pounds. As a result, he could not get a horse that could carry him faster than a walk. So, he did the sensible thing and retired at half pay.

Source: 1. *The Genealogy and History of the Shreve Family from 1641* by L.P. Allen, 1901. 4. New Jersey Marriage Records.

You Think I'm Tough, Wait until You Meet My Daughter

Henry Reynolds was a Quaker and an ardent defender of the cause of the colonies. He even took part as a soldier at the Battle of Stony Point. His outspoken support of the Patriots caused hatred among his Tory neighbors.

Late one night the Tories broke into the Reynold's home and beat Henry. His pregnant wife entered the room and seeing her bleeding husband on the floor went into convulsions. One of the younger children, Caleb, entered the room and was beaten unconscious. Phoebe their daughter who was only eleven at the time fought the men with such fury that it took two Tories to restrain her.

One of the intruders put a rope around Henry's neck and hung him in the living room of the house. Believing him to soon be dead they started to leave. Phoebe quickly cut her father down. The Tories threatened to kill her with a sword, if she did not get away from her father. She was stabbed with the sword, and she promptly threw herself on her father to shield him. She was then beaten with a rope, pulled from her father, and thrown across the room.

Once again the Tories put the rope around Henry's neck and hung him. As they were leaving Phoebe again released him and threw herself on her father to protect him. Twice Phoebe was stabbed. The Tories took her father and threw him into a chest and closed the lid. Then, they looted the house and left.

Phoebe, now covered with blood, attempted to remove her father from the chest. Her mother had recovered and helped her get Henry out of the chest and onto the bed. Both were relieved when Henry's groan indicated he was still alive.

While Phoebe administered aid to her father, her mother shouted, *"Oh, Phoebe! Phoebe! The house is on fire in three places! And I can't put it out, if it burns down over our heads."* The Tories had set fire to some flax and to two straw beds. Phoebe managed to put the fire out and tried to make her brother Caleb go to the neighbors for help. The poor injured boy was frozen with fear and would not budge. So, Phoebe left her home and started out to give the alarm to her neighbors. She warned her neighbors of the Tories, and a doctor was sent to the Reynold's farm. A group of armed settlers took out after the band of Tories.

Henry had over thirty wounds and fortunately none had hit a vital organ. One of his ears was nearly severed from his head, and one arm was so badly injured that he never regained use of it.

Sources: 1. *Women Patriots of the American Revolution: a Biographical Dictionary* by Charles E. Claghorn. 2. New York Times Article December 7, 1879.

Who Spiked the Cannon?

When an army retreats and there is a danger of their cannons falling into the hands of the enemy they will spike their cannons so they cannot be used again until the spike is removed. It takes great difficulty to remove this spike. To spike a cannon you hammer a barbed steel spike into the touch-hold of the cannon. The touch hold is a small hole near the rear of the cannon, where the explosion or ignition of the charge occurs.

Preserved Clapp was a very ingenious soldier that invented a machine that could restore the use of the cannon. For this valuable service he was paid out of the state treasury.

Sources: 1. D.A.R. Lineage Book, Vol.102, page 174. 2. *Record of the Clapp Family in America* by Ebenezer Clapp, 1876.

You Can't Make Me Talk

Philip McArthur was too young at the beginning of the Revolution to serve in the army. His father and several brothers served in a South Carolina Regiment. One day while taking provisions to his father, Philip was captured by some Tories. They demanded that the boy divulge where his father and his Regiment were. He refused to talk, so the Tories strung him up from a tree limb. They continued to question him, and Philip although near death still refused to give them answers. Finally, the officer in charge cursed at the boy and ordered him cut down. He told his men that the lad would die before he would tell them what they wanted to know.

Source: 1. *Revolutionary Reader, Reminiscences and Indian Legends* by Sophie Lee Foster, page, 131.

The Moonlight Makes Me Look Older

Deborah Champion was about twenty-two when her father asked her to ride over a hundred miles through enemy territory to deliver dispatches and army payroll to General Washington. She was stopped by a British soldier, and she pulled the hood of her coat down to cover her face. The soldier mistook her for an old woman, and he let her go on to Boston.

Sources: 1. D.A.R. Lineage Book, Vol. 28, page 270. 2. *The Pioneer Mothers of America* by Harry Clinton Green, Mary Wolcott Green.

Just Out for a Sunday Ride, Nearly Every Day

Red-haired Ann Simpson was an excellent horsewoman, so it was not unusual for her Tory neighbors to see her riding around the country side. At the age of fifteen she was handpicked by General Washington to carry messages to his generals while the army was in eastern Pennsylvania. Many times she carried messages smuggled in sacks of grain and vegetables, sometimes in bullets, and in her clothing. Often she would deliver these messages at the various mills in and around the area. At times she would dress as an old woman, and more than once she had to swallow the messages when she was going to be searched.

Her service ended when General Washington left her area. Because she displayed uncommon bravery she received a letter of Commendation from Washington thanking her for her service.

Sources: 1. The Ann Simpson Davis Chapter, Daughters of the American Revolution. 2. Sons of the American Revolution Application. 3. Tombstone. 4. *Women Patriots of the American Revolution: a Biographical Dictionary* by Charles E. Claghorn.

Make up Your mind, Are You Going to Hang Me or Not?

Benjamin Mayes, nicknamed Daddy Ben, was a royal prince in Africa. He was brought to America and sold to Colonel Scott. During the Revolution the British wanted to find Colonel Scott. They could not find him, but they did capture Mayes. In an attempt to get him to reveal the whereabouts of Scott, the British hung Mayes and cut him down before he was dead. They did this not once but three times. Despite this torture, Mayes refused to divulge his master's hiding place. Mayes for his bravery and loyalty was awarded a gold medal by the people of Maury County, Tennessee.

Source: *Black Heroes and Founders of the Great American Revolution*, posted by iusbvision.

Thanks, But I'll Sleep with My Clothes On

Many women served in the Revolutionary War. Most were camp followers who accompanied their husbands or family members. Some of these women sought adventure or were in search of a living. Most were involved in cooking, nursing, or doing wash. Occasionally, they fought alongside the men and were usually dressed as men. Such was the case of Anna Maria Lane, who wore the clothing of a soldier and was wounded performing her duties during the Battle of Germantown. Even though they were dressed as men, they did not pass themselves off as males. There was no doubt in anyone's eyes that they were females.

Some women, however, went a step further. They disguised themselves as men and fought along with the soldiers. They knew that if they were discovered, they would be removed from the ranks and could face jail time.

Ann (Nancy) Bailey enlisted in 1777 under the name of Samuel Gay. She served in the 1st Massachusetts Regiment, and in just a few weeks she was promoted to the rank of Corporal. After three weeks, for reasons known only to her, she deserted. Her company Commander Captain Abraham Hunt swore out a warrant for her arrest. She was soon captured and discovered to be a woman. She was fined by a civilian court for *"appearing in men's clothing,"* and she was sentenced to two months in prison.

A young New Jersey woman enlisted as a male in 1778 and was discovered almost at once. She was ordered to march through town while being humiliated by soldiers and townspeople.

Sally St. Clair disguised herself as a man and served in a South Carolina Regiment. It was reported that she fought alongside either her husband or boyfriend. They were both killed in the same battle. Her true identity was not discovered until her death.

The most famous of the impersonators was Deborah Sampson. She enlisted under the name of Robert Shurtliff and served for seventeen months. She was wounded twice in battle and her secret was not discovered until she was taken ill with a fever in 1783. She was given an honorable discharge and later awarded a pension for her service.

Sources: 1. *Ann Bailey: Mystery Woman Warrior of 1777* by Patrick J. Leonard, MINERVA: Quarterly Report on Women and the Military, Vol. XI Nos. 3 & 4. 2. *America's First Woman Warrior: the Courage of Deborah Sampson* by Lucy Freeman and Alma Bond. 3. *Battle Cries and Lullabies* by Linda Grant DePauw.

I'm Glad You Asked

Anna Elliott was walking with a British officer in her garden in South Carolina one day. The officer, noted for his cruelty and relentless persecution of those opposed to his political views, pointed to a chamomile and asked what kind of flower it was. Anna said, *"It's called a rebel flower."* The officer asked why it was called that. Anna replied, *"Because, it always flourishes most when trampled upon."*

Source: 1. *Daughters of America on Women of the Century* by Phebe A. Hannafore, 1883.

I Pretended That He Was a British Soldier

Charles Gowens served In the Virginia militia during the Revolution. He lived to be 106 and at the age of 103 he won a squirrel shooting contest.

Source: 1. The Gowen Family Tree Newsletter 6 June, 1998.

Last Man Standing

Many historians believe that Lemuel Cook, who died at the age of 107 in 1866 was the last surviving American soldier of the American Revolution. According to pension records the true last survivor was not Lemuel, but Daniel F. Bakeman who died April 5, 1869. The mistake was due to the fact that Daniel did not receive a pension until he was 107 in 1867. His first pension application was rejected, and in 1867 he was awarded a pension for his service by a special act of Congress.

Daniel joined the army around the age of seventeen and served the last four years of the war in Colonel Willett's Regiment. Many years later he heard of the surrender of Lee at Appomattox and read of the purchase of Alaska from Russia.

After he received his pension, Daniel was invited by neighboring towns to ride in their Fourth of July parades. He would go to each town, fire a salute, and yell, *"Hurrah for Washington, Putnam, Gates, and Lee and all of the brave soldiers who fought for Liberty."* He said he voted in every presidential election, voting first for George Washington and the last time for General Grant.

He was never too old to enjoy a good joke. When Daniel was in his 90's he and some men were digging a well and were about sixteen feet down when the dinner bell rang. The men left Daniel in the well and went to eat. Soon after they began eating he walked in. They never found out how he climbed out of the well, and he left them guessing.

Source: Pension Papers S17265.

The Dirty Look

Chaplain David Sanford had a commanding personal appearance, an impulsive fearless spirit, and he had the power of expression in merely a look. An example of the powerful look was demonstrated once, while he was preaching to the troops in a run-down church.

During his sermon a board that had been placed in one of the shattered windows blew down. The soldiers made so much noise trying to put the board back up, that David had to stop his sermon. Soon the board again blew in, and again the soldiers made a racket trying to put the board back up. When the board fell down a third time, and the soldiers rushed to it to put it back up, Pastor Sanford had enough of the noise. He thundered out, *"let that board alone!"* Immediately the startled men returned to their seats.

After the service a local citizen asked the commanding officer how he liked the preacher. He replied, *"Very well, but I should have liked him better if he hadn't sworn so." "Sworn Captain?"* said the citizen, *"I didn't hear any oath."* The Captain replied, *"Yes he did."* He said, *"let that board alone."* The citizen told the Captain that that was not an oath. *"Well,"* said the Captain, *"if he did not say those very words he looked them."* This later became a bye-word, so whenever a preacher saw another preacher give a strong frown of displeasure, they would say good-naturedly, *"don't swear so."*

Sources: 1. *The Chaplains and Clergy of the Revolution* by Joel Tyler Headley, 1864, pages 361-4. 2. *Yale and Her Honor Roll in the American Revolution* by Henry Phelps Johnston, page 208. 3. D.A.R. Lineage Book, Vol. 16, page 103. 4. Sons of the American Revolution Application.

You Want to Rethink That?

Dicey Langston was a fifteen year old girl that is remembered in history for her daring rides through the countryside carrying messages for the Americans. A little told story about her demonstrates her courage and resolve.

Her brother James, a rebel leader, had left a rifle in her care and told her to keep it until he sent for it. One day a group of men showed up at the Langston home asking for the rifle. Dicey retrieved the rifle, and as she entered back into the room where the men were she remembered that her brother said that if anyone came to claim the rifle they should give a countersign to prove that they were patriots. Dicey did not recognize these men and feared they might be Tories, so she asked for the countersign. One of the men told her it was a little late to be making conditions since the rifle and she were clearly in their possession. Dicey cocked the rifle and pointed it at the man and said, *"If the gun is in your possession, take charge of here!"* The man could tell by her look and the tone of her voice that she meant business. He quickly gave the countersign, and they all had a good laugh. One of the men remarked to Dicey that she was certainly worthy to be called the sister of James Langston.

Sources: 1. *Women Patriots of the American Revolution: a Biographical Dictionary* by Charles E. Claghorn. 2. *The Women of the American Revolution* by Elizabeth F. Ellet, 3rd edition, 1849. 3. *Women in the American Revolution* by Elizabeth, Ellet, 1849.

If I Am Wounded or Sick Don't take Me to the Hospital

Dr. Benjamin Rush said, *"Hospitals are the sinks of human life in the army."* A soldier had a two percent chance of dying in combat, but when admitted to a crowded army hospital the likelihood of death increased to twenty-five percent. One source said that six out of every seven soldier's deaths were due to camp illness. What made hospitals so dangerous?

The sick were laid in long lines side by side on straw beds. Since straw was so scarce, it was never changed or aired and any disease on the straw would be passed on. A patient would have his arms and legs washed, and to prevent head lice his hair would be combed. But little creatures would still be in the straw and the unwashed clothes the soldier had on.

Hospital toilets consisted of pails in the corners of the room and sometimes bedpans if available. Many times the ill were often left to lie in their own filth. Wounds were washed with water that drained into pails, so that it could be reused on other patients.

The sick were usually given soup to eat, because it was believed that solid foods would use up energy needed to fight disease. The soup helped to spread disease, because one spoon was used to feed an entire ward. Leeches were used to remove bad "humors" from a body that may have already lost a large amount of blood.

No one knew that bacteria and viruses caused disease, so there was no need to sterilize instruments used in surgery. Treatment of injuries included a reduced diet, and digestive purges with enemas and diuretics. Large doses of mercury were used to treat many diseases.

After the war surgeon Pierre Francois Percy wrote, *"In retreat before the enemy there is no more frightful a spectacle than the evacuation of mutilated soldiers on big wagons, each jolt bring the most piercing cries. They have to suffer from rain, from suffocating heat or freezing cold, and often do not have aid or food of any sort. Death would be a favor and we have often heard them begging it as a gift from heaven."*

Sources; 1. *Medicine in the American Colonies* by James B. Beck. 2. *Battlefield Angels: Saving Lives under Enemy Fire from Valley Forge to Afghanistan* by Scott McGaugh.

You Don't Whip Me as Hard as by Mamma

The average desertion rate in the Continental Army was 20 to 25 percent. In the latter years of the war the rate went down as the army became more professional. Punishments ranged from various numbers of lashes to death. The average number of lashes for desertion in 1775 was thirty-nine, and the average rose to 100 in 1776.

The guilty soldier was tied to a post and stripped to his waist. Other soldiers were assembled to witness the punishment. A drummer beat the drum to keep cadence to the lashes. After about fifty lashes the man's back became a bloody mess, and a fresh dry whip was then used. If the soldier was to receive a 100 or more lashes, the punishment would be spread out over several days.

Sometimes an excessive number of lashes were ordered. Robert Kennedy of the 8th Pennsylvania received four hundred lashes. He was given three hundred for repeated desertion and an extra 100 for stealing. In 1779 another repeated deserter was given five hundred lashes over a period of time.

Desertion was not the only crime that could result in lashings. They were also given for drunkenness, theft, and the use of profanity.

Very few men deserted because of the fear of getting shot or killed. Cowards did not enlist in the first place. The soldier was serving with his friends and neighbors, and if he deserted how would he be able to face them back home? The deserter would also need to get family or friends to hide him from the people that would come looking for him.

So, what would cause the soldier to desert? Some did because they felt that military punishments in the camp were too harsh or unfair. Some officers would give up to fifty lashes for small and minor infractions. Most soldiers were farmers, so they might desert in the fall or spring because they were needed for planting at home. A failure to plant crops could lead to starvation for their families.

Since there was usually a signing bonus of one or more month's pay for enlisting, some men ran off to join another unit so that they could get more money. One dishonest man did this seven times and was hung for it.

Sources: 1. *Soldiers of Oakham, Massachusetts, in the Revolutionary War* by Henry Parks Wright. 2. *Desertion and the American Soldier, 1776-2006* by Robert Fantina, pages 22-24. 3. *American Revolution: People and Perspectives* edited by Andrew Frank, pages 131-132. 2. *A Military Journal during the American Revolutionary War, from 1775 to 1783* by James Thacher, 1823, pages 222-224.

Twice a Traitor

Benedict Arnold was not the only American soldier to switch to the British side during the war. Joseph Bettys (1754-1782) served as an American soldier in the Revolution, and he was later hanged as a British Spy. After the Battle of Valcour Island he was captured by the British and sent to Canada. During his captivity he switched to the British side and served as a spy.

He was later captured by the Americans, tried, and condemned to be hung at West Point. His parents and many influential people asked that he be released, promising that he would mend his life. General Washington granted his pardon. Once released Joseph rejoined the British and recruited soldiers for them.

Joseph was later tracked down by three men and once again became a prisoner of the Americans. He offered his American captors a considerable amount of gold, if they would allow him to escape. The men refused the bribe, and Joseph was tried as a spy and hung in 1782.

Source: 1. *Daring Deeds of the Old Heroes of the Revolution* by Henry C. Watson, 1893, pages 147-151.

I Also Have Some Swamp Land to Sell

It was not unusual for an officer to trick a young boy, especially if they could not read, into serving extra time in the army. This became necessary because after the first couple of years the war was not going well for the Americans and enlistments began to drop off. Besides the harsh conditions of war, many of the men were not being paid regularly or they were paid in worthless Continental money.

There was one story that a young boy accidently fired his musket in a foxhole, and he was reported to the officer in charge. The officer told him there was severe punishment for this offense, and he could avoid punishment if he extended his enlistment for a year. The boy agreed to extend his enlistment, and he was later told by some of the men that he was tricked by the officer.

Sources: 1. *On This Day: 365 Amazing and Inspiring Stories about Saints, Martyrs, and Heroes* by Robert Morgan. 2. *The Vermont Encyclopedia* by John J. Duffy, Samuel B. Hand, Ralph H. Orth.

Ten Things Wrong with the Painting

The painting of Washington crossing the Delaware was painted in 1851, 75 years after the crossing, and it has several inaccuracies.

National Archives

1. The flag in the painting is the "Starts and Stripes", which did not exist at the time of Washington's Crossing.
2. The boat pictured is too small to carry all occupants and stay afloat. It also has higher sides than depicted.
3. The painting has a bright sky, while the crossing was at midnight.
4. The ice in the river is shown as jagged chucks, yet broad sheets of ice are more common on the Delaware River.
5. The river in the painting looks wide, but the Delaware crossing was at a narrow spot (less than 300 yards).
6. It was raining during the crossing but clear in the painting.
7. Washington is pictured as standing, which would have increased the chance of capsizing the row boat.
8. In the background of the painting you can see horses that are rearing on the rowboats. The horses and cannons were sent across on flat boats.
9. The men in the boat are shown as being very diverse, which was probably not the case. The painting shows 2 farmers with their broad-brimmed hats, an Indian wearing moccasins, pants, and the hat of a Native American. There is a man with a Scottish bonnet, a man of African descent (some historians say his name is Prince Whipple), a future President (some say is James Monroe), and a person without a hat and in a red shirt that many historians say represent a woman.
10. At the time of the crossing many of the Americans had rags for uniforms and many had no shoes, but just their feet wrapped. In the painting all the people have shoes and nice clothing.

Sources: 1. *Washington's Crossing* by David Hackett Fischer. 2. *Crossing the Delaware, More Accurately* by Corey Kilgannon.

Can You Spare $80 Dollars for a Cup of Coffee?

Once the war began gold and silver coins were scarce. Each state printed its own money to pay for the war, and because so much was printed and it was easy to copy, the paper money lost most of its value. When one soldier was paid eighty dollars Continental money, the dollar was worth less than ¼ of a cent. It was just enough money to pay for breakfast and a bit of rum. Many people called the money *"shin plasters,"* because they felt the only use it had was to bandage a sore leg.

Source: 1. *Dictionary of Americanisms: A Glossary of Words and Phrases Usually Regarded as Peculiar to the United States* by John Russell Barlett, page 402.

There Will be No Refund for the Cloth

Joshua Prewett was a soldier in the Revolution, and his wife Mary wanted to apply to the government for a widow's pension. When a widow applied for her deceased husband's pension, she had to show proof of death. This was usually achieved by having several people send a letter attesting to the fact that they attended the funeral of the person. Mary had a most unusual letter sent by John Stollstein as proof of her husband's death. John was a merchant, and he said he sold Mary several yards of material to use as shrouding for the funeral of her husband. The total cost was $2.10, and he said would be happy to show his books of purchase as proof.

Sources: 1. Pension Papers of Joshua Prewett W27643.

I Also Hear Voices

John Aitkin (John the Painter) was a small time criminal in Edinburgh, Scotland. When it seemed that he might get arrested he became an indentured servant (agreed to work for someone in exchange for passage to America), and he left for Jamestown, Virginia. He had no desire to work for a number of years to pay for his passage, so he escaped to North Carolina. For the next few years he bounced around between New York City, Boston, Philadelphia, and New Jersey.

He claimed that while living in New Jersey the British treated him poorly and suspected him of siding with the patriots. They burned down his house, which he considered to be an insult. He was determined to get revenge and decided that he would kill King George. He thought that by striking a blow against England he would be recognized and rewarded by the Americans.

He traveled to Paris where he met with the American diplomat Silas Deanne. John told Deane about his assassination plans. Deane reasoned with him and suggested that it was mean and cowardly to attempt to assassinate a man in cold blood. He told John that if he wanted revenge he should do it in a *"manly, generous way."*

John agreed and devised another plan for revenge. Now his plan was to destroy British ships in the harbors and dockyards in England. Using his knowledge of mixing chemicals and paint solvents from his trade as a painter, John would make incendiary devices to burn buildings in the Royal Dockyards. For the next several months John did attack facilities in Portsmouth and Bristol, but he caused little damage. Other fires during this time were incorrectly attributed to him, which speeded up efforts to capture him. A landlady he rented a room from became suspicious of him and alerted authorities.

John was soon arrested, tried, and condemned to be hung. He told the authorities that he was ready to die and didn't care how soon. John was hung from the mizzenmast of the HMS *Arethusa*, making his hanging one from the highest gallows ever used. It was estimated that 20,000 people attended the hanging.

Source: 1. *Journal or Historical Recollections of American Events during the Revolutionary War* by Elias Boudinot, 1894.

The Cure Might Kill You

During the Revolutionary War the threat of smallpox was a major concern for the army. Most British soldiers had already been exposed and were immune. Unfortunately, the Colonial troops were not. Medics would create a small wound in the healthy soldier's arm, and then they would rub some of the pus from the pox of an infected soldier into that wound. This would give him a slight case of the pox, and then he would be immune. This early method of inoculation had been learned from African slaves.

Since they had no way to control the dosage, there was danger involved. If you received too large a dose you could die. Washington estimated that as many as two percent of inoculated soldiers could die. Without the inoculation more than one third of the soldiers could die, and another third would be too ill to fight if an outbreak occurred. Washington had his troops inoculated during their stay at Valley Forge.

Sources: 1. *Pox Americana: The Great Smallpox Epidemic of 1775-82* by Elizabeth A. Fenn. 2. *Medicine and the American Revolution* by Oscar Reiss, M.D.

What Would Happen if I Did Something Really Bad?

American soldiers could be subjected to harsh punishment while in camp. The following are examples taken from pension applications,

"One young man was heard by Col. Tolls to say that his time was out and he would go home. Tolls had him put under guard and the next day for his offence he received 25 lashes, four muskets was stacked up with bayonets locked in each other, the young man was tied and hitched to the bayonets, the men were drawn up in a circle to see him whipped—after this although many of us thought we had a right to go home nothing more was said."

Source: 1. Pension Application of James Chick S10440.

"I well remember that a man was stripped and whipped for firing his gun whilst in camp; that he was whipped by the Corporal and I was sorry to see it for he always thought it was an accident in firing the gun."

Source: 1. Pension Application of Robert Chewning R1915.

They Call Me One Punch Isaac

Near the end of the war thirteen year old Isaac Wheeler Jr., being large for his age, engaged in privateering. The ship on which he served was captured by the British, and the captured Americans were placed below decks on the British ship except for Isaac. Because of his young age he was permitted to be on the upper deck. A British Lieutenant who had a pompous attitude and was prone to drink too much took a dislike toward the young boy. Later in the evening the Lieutenant gave the boy a kick and with a curse told Isaac to get out of his way. This anger caused Isaac to knock the man down with a single swing. Isaac was immediately seized and taken below, with the promise that in the morning he would be placed in yardarms. Fortunately, during the night the French retook the ship and Isaac was set free in Chesapeake Bay. Isaac later saw the surrender of Cornwallis at Yorktown.

Sources: 1. Chapter Sketches: Connecticut D.A.R. 2. D.A.R. Magazine, Vol 7, July-December 1897.

Generous George

Harper's Monthly magazine published an anecdote in December of 1864, and it was re-published several times after that. Some historians have serious doubts if the story is true. If it is not true, it should be.

"When Colonel Seth Warner died just after the revolution, his farm was heavily mortgaged. Seth had spent all his energies supporting the Revolution, and the family finances had suffered. Seth's untimely death left his family facing a certain loss of their farm. George Washington, who held Seth Warner in high regard as a Patriot, personally rode to the Warner farm in 1789 and counted out the silver coins to the exact sum required to retire the mortgage and save the farm. Washington wanted this act of Generosity kept a secret."

Source: 1. Harper's Monthly magazine December, 1864.

Smile

The army had various requirements for enlistments. The minimum height requirement was five feet five inches, you had to be fifteen years or older, and you had to have an upper and a lower tooth meet so that you could bite off the top of a cartridge.

The Not So Secret Handshake

Mohawk Chief Thayandanega, who was commonly called Captain Joseph Brant, had been attacking American communities in the upper Delaware Valley. American Captain John Wood was taken prisoner by Brant's warriors and was going to be put to death. By some stroke of luck, Wood accidently gave Brant's hand the Master Mason's grip.

Years earlier Brant had been taken to England and had become a Mason, and he assumed that Wood was a lodge brother. He ordered Wood to be released, thus saving the American's life. Later Wood, who was not a Mason, felt compelled to join the organization.

Sources: 1. *America: Through Revolution to Empire* by Francis Jennings, page 255. 2. D.A.R. Lineage Book, Vols. 59-60, page 147.

I Didn't Know These Things Grew on Bushes

Pastor Charles Cummings was known as a fighter. Because of the fear of Indian attacks he always carried a gun, even to church. Every Sunday he would *"put on his shot-pouch, shoulder his rifle, mount his horse and ride to church."* After placing his weapons within reach, he would preach two sermons with a short interval between.

One story is told how he saved the town from an Indian attack by self-scalping. As the story goes, Indians attacked while the pastor was riding in a wagon, and as he jumped to safety his wig caught in the brush. The Indians were so surprised to see a "scalp" hanging on a limb that they hesitated to attack the town. This provided time for Cummings to organize a defense.

Sources: 1. *Encyclopedia of the Presbyterian Church in the United States of America* by Alfred Nevin, page 653. 2. *The Chaplains and Clergy of the Revolution* by Joel Tyler Headley, 1864, pages 273-275. 3. *Annals of Augusta County* by Jos. A. Waddell, 1886, pages 52-53. 4. *A Popular History of the Presbyterian Church* by Jacob Harris Patton, 1900, page 216.

Dressing for Battle

Joseph Johnson was an Indian fighter in the Revolutionary War from Pennsylvania. In his pension application he described his militia equipment, *"We equip ourselves at our own expence in the following articles, one Rifle Gun, Shot pouch powder Horn, half pound powder, one pound lead run into Bullitts, a knapsack, tomahawk, Scalping knife, Belt and Blankett."*

Source: 1. Pension Application of Joseph Johnson R5639.

****

John Shellman provided a good description of his uniform in his pension application dated 1833. *"A proposition was made by, I believe, Capt. Mantz that the whole Company should volunteer Service, which was immediately acceded to with perhaps a few exceptions. We accordingly prepared by each man furnishing himself with a uniform consisting of a Hunting shirt, dyed yellow with Hickory bark, Pantaloons of the same, a pair of Indian Legons of gran cloth with a piece of Bearskin over the crown of the hat: armed with a good Rifle and Tomahawk, shot pouch & powder horn – thus armed and accoutred, we took up the line of march about the 1st of June for the City of Annapolis."*

Source: Pension application S31960.

****

Zela Reno described his uniform shirt in his pension application dated February of 1833. *"This declarant's uniform was a purple hunting shirt, marked in the breast in large letters with the words "Liberty or death" with a Mecaroni hat & buck tail."*

Source: Pension application W8545.

You Can Keep My Junk Mail

Colonel Timothy Pickering had been in the Revolutionary War since the Battle of Lexington and Concord. He was praised for his work in supplying the troops during the war and in 1780 in was appointed to the important post of Quartermaster General. While at the Siege of Yorktown he ran into a problem. Now keep in mind he had been fighting and sacrificing in this war for six years and he currently held one of the most important positions on Washington's staff.

Congress had allowed some officers free postage during the war. For some reason they denied it to Colonel Pickering while at Yorktown. He could not receive important letters for his job if did not pay the postage. Unfortunately he was short of funds, because like the other soldiers, he had not received any pay for most of the year. Pickering wrote the following letter to Congress while at Yorktown on October 11, 1781,

> Two or three days since, I had the mortification to be refused the letters in the post-office addressed to me, unless I paid the postage. Before that time the postmaster had contented himself with charging me with the postage of letters. Those above referred to were all on public business, and I wished to take them up; but want of money obliged me to leave them in office, where they still remain.
>
> I entreat the attention of Congress on this subject. Certain officers of the army receive their letters free from postage. The letters of the principal staff must generally be at least as necessary and important; I cannot even conjecture one tolerable reason for the distinction. Nor can I discern any public advantage in the regulation obliging the latter to pay for public letters. As the matter now stands, I must either obtain any letters by the post, without payment, or, if this be inadmissible, I shall be obliged to direct all my deputies to cease sending me any paper by the post, and to suspend their communication till other conveyances present.

On October 22nd the letter was read to Congress and it was resolved, "That letters to and from the Quartermaster General be carried free of postage."

Source: Pickering, Octavius, *The Life of Timothy Pickering, Vol. I* by Octavius Pickering, pages 306-307.

Chapter 8

"It is yet to be decided whether the Revolution must ultimately be considered as a blessing or a curse: a blessing or a curse, not to the present age alone, for with our fate will the destiny of unborn millions be involved."
----George Washington 1783

Notable Facts of the Revolutionary War

Sampson Coburn, a former slave, joined the Massachusetts Militia and served at the Battle of Bunker Hill. He was later promoted to the rank of Corporal, which was the highest rank given to African Americans and Native Americans.

Sources: 1. Biographies of Patriots of Color at the Battle of Bunker Hill from National Park Service, page 7. 2. *Patriots of Color* by George Quintal Jr. page 85.

****

Pastor William Emerson Sr. tended to the wounded men at the Battle of Concord. With this act he became the first Army chaplain and he later served until September of 1776. While in the army he became ill and was released from his duties to return home. On the way home he died of the fever and became the first chaplain to die while in the service.

Sources: 1. Sons of the American Revolution Application. 2. D.A.R. Lineage Book, Vol. 12, page 224. 3. *With Fire and Sword: The Battle of Bunker Hill and the Beginning of the American Revolution* by James L. Nelson, page 140.

****

The Penobscot Expedition was a 4,000 men naval expedition in the Revolutionary War. It consisted of nineteen warships, twenty-four transport ships, and more than 1,000 militiamen. The purpose of the expedition was to capture a 750 men British garrison on the Penobscot Peninsula in Maine. It ended as a great British victory, and it was the worst U.S. naval defeat until Pearl Harbor in December of 1941. The Americans lost numerous ships and over 470 men, while the British lost only thirteen men.

Source: 1. *Redcoats and Rebels: The American Revolutionary War* by Hugh Bicheno.

****

Rev. John Wesley Gilbert Nevelling converted all his property into money, which amounted to about 5,000 pounds. He loaned it to the American government during the revolution, but he later lost the receipt and was never repaid. He served as a chaplain in New Jersey and died in poverty.

Source: 1. *"The United States Army Chaplaincy by United States Department of the Army. Office of the Chief of Chaplains."* Published 1977.

****

When his brother Nathan was hung as a spy on September 22, 1776, Rev. Enoch Hale joined the army at White Plains and became a chaplain to the regiment recruited near his home.

Sources: 1. D.A.R. Lineage book, Vol. 5, page 86. 2. *"The United States Army Chaplaincy by United States Department of the Army. Office of the Chief of Chaplains."* Published 1977.

****

Joshua Barney had the distinction of being captured by the British six times and once escaped from the infamous Old Mill Prison in Portsmouth, England. Barney who was born in 1759 went to sea at the age of eleven, and at the age of fifteen he commanded a merchant ship when the captain of the ship died. In 1779 he was captured and imprisoned in Old Mill Prison until his escape in 1781. He later achieved the rank of Commodore in the United States Navy, and he served in the War of 1812.

Sources: 1. D.A.R. Lineage Book, Vol.2, page 247. 2. *Biographical Memoir of the late Commodore Joshua Barney* edited by Marv Barney, 1832.

****

George Taylor had twelve sons and no daughters and he may hold the record for the most sons in the Revolutionary War at ten. His first born son George died in 1761 during the French and Indian War. His last son he had by a different wife, also named George and he was thirteen when the war ended. The ten boys that were: 1. James a Sergeant Major in the Virginia line, 2. Jonathan a Lieutenant in the Virginia Guards, 3. Edmund a Captain in the Virginia Militia, 4. Francis a Major in the 5th Virginia, 5. Richard a Captain in the Virginia Navy, 6. William a Major in the Virginia Regulars, 7. Dr. Charles a surgeon in the Virginia Line, 8. Reuben a Captain in the Virginia Regulars, 9. Benjamin a Midshipman in the Virginia Navy, and 10. John a Lieutenant in the Virginia Navy, he was the only son to die in the war. He died on a prison ship in New York.

Sources: 1. D.A.R. Lineage Book, Vol. 63, page 258. 2. Sons of the American Revolution Application.

****

Peter Snell may have the unfortunate distinction of having the most brothers killed in the same battle of the Revolutionary War. Peter and his six brothers served in the 2nd Regiment of the New York Tryon County Militia at the Battle of Oriskany on August 6, 1777. Peter was the only survivor of the seven brothers. There were a total of fourteen Snells that took part in the battle.

Sources: 1. D.A.R. Lineage Book, Vol. 42, page 17. 2. *History of the Mohawk Valley: Gateway to the West 1614-1925* edited by Nelson Greene. 3. Sons of the American Revolution Application.

****

Roger Nelson ran away from home at the age of sixteen and joined a troop of horse, under the command of Colonel William Augustine Washington. He was captured at the surrender of Charleston and sent to a prison ship in the harbor. After he was exchanged he joined the Maryland Line, and he was in the battles of Eutaw, Guilford, and Camden. There he was left on the field for dead and again was imprisoned. He was exchanged and remained in the service until the war ended. He may have been the most wounded soldier in the war, because he had sixteen wounds upon his body. He later attained the rank of Brigadier General.

Source: 1. D.A.R. Lineage Book, Vol. 2, page 284.

****

The last American wounded during the fighting at the Battles of Lexington and Concord was Caesar Augustus, who was a black servant of Mr. Tileston of Dorchester, Massachusetts. As the British were retreating back to Boston, Caesar was seen firing at them and was wounded near a house close to Charlestown. He was taken prisoner, and exchanged on June 5, 1775 with several other American prisoners.

Sources: 1. *Patriots of Color* by George Quintal Jr. page 55. 2. Forgotten Patriots, National Society of the D.A.R., page 100.

****

At the time of the Revolutionary War about 20% of the Colonial population of twenty-two million were black and the number of blacks that fought for the Americans was over 5,000. By 1779 15% of the army was black. These men served in an integrated army, which would be the last one until the Korean War.

****

The average height of American men in the Revolutionary War was 5 feet 8 inches, which was about three inches taller than the British soldier. Amos Parker was considered to be the tallest American soldier standing at almost eight feet tall. During a battle he saved the life of General Lafayette.

Source: 1. *Biographical and Portrait Cyclopedia of Chautauqua County, New York* by Obed Edison.

****

American General Lincoln visited the army while it was camped on the Savannah, and was given a thirteen gun salute in his honor. One of the soldiers was killed when he was in the act of ramming down the cartridge.

Source: 1. Pension Application of Cannon Carson S21103.

****

Pastor John Ellis served as a chaplain from July 6, 1775 until October 31, 1783 making him the longest serving chaplain in the Revolutionary war.

Source: 1. *Chaplains of the Revolutionary War: Black Robed American Warriors* by Jack Darrell Crowder.

****

Ripley's Believe it or Not wrote that Colonel Hans Christian Febiger is known as the only soldier who took part in every important battle of the Revolution from Bunker Hill to Yorktown.

Source: 1. Ripley's Believe it or Not! February 20, 1942.

****

James Morgan of the 1st Company of the 8th Regiment of Connecticut Militia was wounded at the Battle of Fort Griswold on September 6, 1781. He probably set the number of bayonet wounds a soldier received in one battle, he survive with 15 wounds. According to his pension application he *"was wounded in the left shoulder, and breast, and in sundry parts of his body by a bayonet."* James received the impressive amount of $4 a month disability for his fifteen wounds.

Sources: 1. D.A.R. Lineage Book, Vol. 9, page 352. 2. Pension Application S20887 for James Morgan.

****

More than 11,000 Americans died on the sixteen British prison ships from 1776 to 1783. This was three times greater than the number of men who died in combat.

Sources: 1. *American Prisoners of the Revolution* by Danske Dandridge. 2. *Forgotten Patriots, the Untold Story of American Prisoners during the Revolutionary War* by Edwin G. Burrows.

****

At the Battle of Princeton on January 3, 1777, Captain Stephen Olney saved the life of the future President James Monroe.

Source: 1. *Biography of Revolutionary Heroes* by Catherine Williams, 1839, pages 199-200.

****

The Battle of Short Hills took place in New Jersey on June 26, 1777. It was reported that some troops from both sides used poisoned musket balls dipped in fungus.

Sources 1. *The Battle of the Short Hills* by Robert A. Mayers, GardenStateLegacy.com, Issue 13, September 2011.

****

During the war when an American soldier was captured he was sometimes released, if he gave his word he would not rejoin the army. John Rutherford was one of more than 2,800 American soldiers captured at the Battle of Fort Washington on November 16, 1776. At the time of exchange John had to swear an oath not to enter the army again. He did not swear not to enter the navy, which he then did.

Sources: 1. Sons of the American Revolution Application. 2. Pension Papers W26422.

****

The Continental Congress adopted the stars and stripes flag on June 14, 1777. The first time that the flag was flown was at Fort Stanwix (also called Fort Schuyler) on August 3, 1777. When Massachusetts reinforcements arrived at the fort, they brought the news of the flag's adoption.

The soldiers cut off their shirts to make the white stripes, the red stripes were made from the red flannel petticoats of the officer's wives. The blue area was made from Captain Swartwout's blue cloth coat. Three days later on October 6 the flag was flown under fire for the first time at the Battle of Oriskany.

Sources: 1. *Naval Ceremonies, Customs, and Traditions* by Connell and Mack, 1934. 2. D.A.R. Lineage Book, Vol. 4, page 216.

****

Nathan Futrell was born on September 10, 1773 in Northampton County, North Carolina, and he is reputed to be the youngest drummer boy at the age of seven to serve in the Revolutionary War. His service was probably short lived because of his age and because he was a member of the militia.

He married Charity Futrell about 1797 in Northampton County, North Carolina. Among her papers was a small yellow slip of paper with the following inscription, *"Jany. 3, 1829, My Consorte Nathan Futrell, served as a drummer player in the North Carolina Militia during the Revolution at the age of seven years. Signed: Charity Futrell."*

Young boys were recruited to act as drummers. The drums played an important part in communicating on the battlefield. The various drum roles signaled different commands from the officers to the troops. At times the boys were treated as mascots by the adult soldiers. Sometimes the youngest boys received no pay but were given money by the officers. About 200 drummers served in the Revolution. The average age was around twenty and with only a few below the age of fourteen.

They would sometimes have other duties during the day. They might serve or wait upon an officer, chop wood, or help the surgeon during sick call. At times they would march out with the fifes in front of the regiment and play a tune before the battle began.

Sources: 1. *Echoes from The Past* by Judy Maupin, a Column of Historical and Genealogical Anecdotes, Stories and Family Notes. Calloway County, Kentucky 2. CD185-Genealogies of Kentucky Families. 3. Vol III, Kentucky Land Grants Vol. 1 pg. 4. Kentucky historical marker. 5. *The Beats of Battle: Images of Army Drummer Boys Endure* by Elizabeth M. Collins, Soldiers The Official U.S. Army Magazine. 6. U.S. Civil War History & Genealogy-The Drummer Boys, genelogyforum.com.

****

George Washington was noted as a modest man. He was having dinner on October 22, 1776 with sixty-one year old Captain Roger Lyon and his wife Mary. The Captain, who was blind, handed a drinking cup to Washington and remarked, *"General, the ladies say that you are a handsome man, but I cannot see."* Washington took the cup and replied, *"Tell the ladies I am afraid they are as blind as yourself."*

Source: 1. *Women Patriots of the American Revolution: a Biographical Dictionary* by Charles E. Claghorn, page 128.

****

Captain William Clark led a company of men at the Battle of Eutaw Springs on September 8, 1781. During the battle he killed a British officer which he regretted for the rest of his life, and could not speak of it without shedding tears.

Clark's son said in his father's pension application, *"He and the officer he killed were engaged in dressing the lines of their respective companies, preparatory to entering into the battle, when he took a gun out of the hands of one of his men, shot at the British officer and saw him fall."*

Captain Clark considered this a murderous act, since neither of their companies were then engaged in the battle. Years later Clark became a member of the Quaker Society. When he was urged to apply for a pension he usually replied that he would not receive pay for acts which his conscience condemn. William's son filed for his pension in 1845, which was rejected.

Source: 1. Pension file R1968.

****

Most soldiers when they are discharged receive their papers and they start walking home. According to the pension application of Private John Miles his discharge was a little unusual. *"When my term of three months expired and my discharge was given to me by Col. Richard Casewell; previous to discharging his soldiers, at the request of the citizens of New Bern, he carried them all about one mile from the town and giving them their discharges he unheaded a barrel of rum and told them to help themselves."* This author wonders how many of the men got lost walking home after they drank their fill.

Source: 1. Pension Application S21376 of John Miles.

****

Richard Roberts served in the army, and was present at several battles including the surrender of Lord Cornwallis. In Richard's pension application he told of two strange and interesting stories.

The first story occurred when he was stationed at the lead mines in Wythe County, Virginia, *"......there was a noise heard from the station like the yelping of a Turky – one of the soldiers went out to shoot it – a gun was heard – and it was supposed he had killed the Turkey – but not returning as soon as expected – they went to see the cause – found him dead, instead of the Turkey – the noise being made by the Indians who killed him – to decoy him out &c."*

The second story happen during the Siege of Yorktown in 1781, *"One of the Soldiers saw a cannon ball or bomb coming, and struck it with his spade, and it broke every bone in his arm."*

Source: Pension application W4573.

****

Sometimes just the force from the wind of a passing cannon shot can cause injury. Doctor Thacher, was examining a wounded soldier at the Battle of Springfield in 1780, recorded that the soldier's *"arm was fractured above the elbow, without the smallest perceptible injury to his clothes, or contusion or discoloration of skin. He made no complaint, but I observed he was feeble and a little confused in his mind. He received proper attention but expired the next day. The idea of injury by the wind of a ball, I learn, is not new, instances of the kind have, it is said, occurred in naval battles, and are almost constantly attended with fatal effects."*

Source: *A Military Journal during the American Revolutionary War, from 1775 to 1783.* By Dr. James Thacher page 241.

Bibliography

Publications:

Aiken, Scott, *The Swamp Fox: Lessons in Leadership from the Partisan Campaigns of Francis Marion.* Annapolis, Maryland: Naval Institute Press, 2012.

Allen, L.P., *The Genealogy and History of the Shreve Family from 1641.* Greenville, Illinois: Privately Printed, 1901.

_____, *American Revolutionary Soldiers of Franklin County, Pennsylvania.* Historical Works Committee of the Franklin County Chapter, 1944.

Anderson, Lee Patrick, *Forgotten Patriot: The life and Times of Major-General Nathanael Greene.* Irvine, California: Universal Publishers, 2002.

Anderson, Lee Patrick, *Forty Minutes by the Delaware "The Battle of Fort Mercer".* Irvine, California: Universal Publishers, 1990.

The Ann Simpson Davis Chapter, Daughters of the American Revolution.

Antal, John, *7 Leadership Lessons of the American Revolution.* Havertown, Pennsylvania: Casemate, 2013.

Barlett, John Russell, *A Glossary of Words & Phrases Usually Relating to the U.S.,* Boston, Massachusetts: Little & Brown, 1860.

Barney, Edna, *So Obscure a Person.* Springfield, Virginia: Barneykin Press, 2008.

Barney, Marv, editor, *Biographical Memoir of the late Commodore Joshua Barney.* Boston, Massachusetts: Gray & Bowen, 1832.

Beck, James B., *Medicine in the American Colonies.* Albany, New York: 1850.

Berg, Fred Anderson, *Encyclopedia of Continental Army Units: Battalions, Regiments, and Independent Corps.* Mechanicsburg, Pennsylvania: Stackpole Books, 1972.

Beveridge, Albert Jeremiah, *The Life of John Marshall.* Boston & New York: Houghton Mifflin, 1916.

Bicheno, Hugh, *Redcoats and Rebels: The American Revolutionary War.* Great Britain: Grafton Books, 1990.

_____, *Black Heroes and Founders of the Great American Revolution,* posted by iusbvision on January 24, 2011.

Boher, Melissa Lukeman, *Glory, Passion, and Principle: the Story of Eight Remarkable women at the Core of the American Revolution.* New York, New York: Atria, 2013.

Boogher, William Fletcher, *Gleanings of Virginia History.* Washington D.C.: W.F. Boogher, 1903.

Boucher, John Newton, *History of Westmoreland County, Pennsylvania, Vol.* New York, New York: Lewis Publishing Co., 1906.

Boudinot, Elias, *Journal or Historical Recollections of American Events during the Revolutionary War.* Trenton, New Jersey: C.L. Traver, 1890.

_____, Boy's Life, Feb. 1956 Vol. 46, No. 2.

Brace, Jeffery, *The Blind African Slave or Memories of Boyrereau Brinch, Nick-Named Jeffrey Brace.* St. Albans, Vermont: Harry Whitney, 1810.

Brooks, Noah, *Henry Knox A Soldier of the Revolution.* New York, New York: G.P. Putman and Sons, 1900.

Buell, Augustus C., *A History of Andrew Jackson.* New York, New York: Charles Scribner's & Sons, 1904.

Bunce, Oliver Bell, *The Romance of the Revolution Being True Stories of Adventure, Romantic Incidences, Hairbreadth Escapes, and Heroic Exploits of the Days of '76.* Philadelphia, Pennsylvania: Porter and Coats, 1870.

Burgan, Michael, *The Untold Story of the Black Regiment: Fighting in the Revolutionary War*. North Mankato, Minnesota: Compass Point Books, 2015.

Burrows, Edwin G., *Forgotten Patriots, the Untold Story of American Prisoners During the Revolutionary War*. New York, New York: Basic Books, 2008.

Byerly, Thomas and Joseph Clinton Robertson, *The Percy Anecdotes*. New York, New York: Myers & Smith, 1822.

Byrd, James P., *Sacred Scripture, Sacred War*. New York, New York: Oxford Press, 2013.

Carrington, Henry Beebee, *Battles of the American Revolution, 1775-1781*. New York, New York: A.S. Barnes & Co. 1876.

Carter, Brent A., *Untamed Leadership: A Journey Through the Instincts that Shape Us*. Enso Books, 2011.

Claghorn, Charles E., *Women Patriots of the American Revolution: a Biographical Dictionary*. Metuchen, New Jersey: The Scarecrow Press, 1991.

Clapp, Ebenezer, *Record of the Clapp Family in America*. Boston, Massachusetts: Clapp & Son, 1876.

Coburn, Frank Warren, *The Battle of April 19, 1775, in Lexington, Concord, Lincoln, Arlington, Cambridge, Somerville and Charlestown*. Lexington, Massachusetts: Published by the Author, 1912.

Coggins, Jack, *Ships and Seamen of the American Revolution*. Mineola, New York: Dover Publications, 1969.

_____, *Collections of the Piscataquis County Historical Society*. Issue 1 by Piscataquis County Historical Society, Dover, Maine.

Collins, Elizabeth M., *The Beats of Battle: Images of Army Drummer Boys Endure*. Soldiers The Official U.S. Army Magazine, 2013.

Cook, Frederick, *Journals of the Military Expedition of Major General John Sullivan*. (Section about Rev. William Rogers) Auburn, New York: Knapp, Peck, & Thompson, 1887.

Compton-Hall, Richard, *The Submarine Pioneers*. England: Periscope Publishing, 1983.

Connell, Royal W. and William P. Mack, *Naval Ceremonies, Customs, and Traditions*. 1934.

Coulter, E. Merton, *Nancy Hart, Georgia Heroine of the Revolution: The Story of the Growth of a Tradition*. Georgia Historical Quarterly 39, June 1955.

Culler, Maurice R., *Battle Road: Birthplace of the American Revolution*. New York, New York: Viking Press, 1970.
Cummings, Alma, *Burials and Inscriptions in the Walnut Street Cemetery*. Brookline, Massachusetts: The Riverdale Press, 1920.

Cunningham, John T., *This is New Jersey*. New Brunswick, New Jersey: Rutgers University Press, 1994.

Current, Richard M., *That Other Declaration: May 20, 1775*. North Carolina Historical Review, Vol. 54, No. 2, April, 1977.

Custis, George Washington Parke, *Recollections and Private Memoirs of Washington by his Adopted Son George Washington Parke Custis*. New York, New York: Derby & Jackson, 1860.

Cutter, William Richard and Benjamin Cutter, *History of the Town of Arlington 1635-1879*. Boston, Massachusetts: David Clapp & Son, 1898.

Cutter, William Richard, editor, *New England Families, Genealogical and Memorial, Vol 2*, New York, New York: Lewis Publishing, 1913.

Cuyler, Chaplain Stanley, *The Chaplains and Clergy at the Battle of Monmouth*. U.S. Army Chaplain Center and School Library, 1986.

Dandridge, Danske, *American Prisoners of the Revolution*. Charlottesville, Virginia: Michie Company, 1911.

_____, D.A.R. Magazine: American Monthly, Vol. 17, 1900.

_____, D.A.R. Magazine: American Monthly, Vol 7, July-December 1897.

Daughters of the American Revolution, *Lineage Book*. Washington D.C.

Daughters of the American Revolution Magazine Vol. 46, Pennsylvania's Patriotic Women during the Revolution.

Delgado, Sarah Hazel, *Descendants and Related Families of David Samuel Ware and Amanda Roelee Chesteen*. Decorah, Iowa: Amundsen Publishing Co., 1985.

DePauw, Linda Grant, *Battle Cries and Lullabies*. Norman, Oklahoma: University of Oklahoma Press, 1998.

DeSaussure, General Wilmot, *An Account of the Siege of Charleston, South Carolina, in 1780*. Charleston, South Carolina: The News and Courier Book Press, 1885.

Diamant, Lincoln, editor, *Revolutionary Women: In the War for American Independence*. West Port, Connecticut: Praeger, 1998.

_____, *Dictionary of American Biography, 1936, 9:336*. New York, New York: C. Scribner's Sons, 1936.

Dolle, Raymond F., *Yankee Doodle and the Country Dance from Lexington to Yorktown*.

Doyle, Joseph B., *Frederick William Von Steuben and the American Revolution*. Steubenville, Ohio: The N. B. Cook Co., 1913.

Drake, Francis S., *Life and Correspondence of Henry Knox*. Boston, Massachusetts: Samuel G. Drake, 1873.

Drimmer, Frederick, *Captured by the Indians: 15 Firsthand Accounts, 1750-1870*. New York, New York: Dover, 1961.

Duffy, John J., Samuel B. Hand, and Ralph H. Orth, *The Vermont Encyclopedia*. Burlington, Vermont: University of Vermont Press, 2003.

Dunkerly, Robert M. and Irene B. Boland. *Eutaw Springs: The Final Battle of the American Revolution's Southern Campaign*. Columbia, South Carolina: University of South Carolina Press, 2017.

Eaton, Hon. Lilley, *Genealogical History of the Town of Reading, Mass*. Boston, Massachusetts: Alfred Mudge & Sons, 1874.

Edison, Obed, *Biographical and Portrait Cyclopedia of Chautauqua County, New York*. Philadelphia, Pennsylvania: Jas. L. Rodgers, 1891.

Elder, CSM Dan, *Remarkable Sergeants: Ten Vignettes of Noteworthy NCOs*. Fort Riley, Kansas: 2008.

Elizabeth Zane Chapter, West Virginia State Society, D.A.R. website.

Ellet, Elizabeth Fries, *The Women of the American Revolution, Vol. 2*. New York, New York: Baker & Scribner, 1848.

Endicott, Charles M., *Account of Leslie's Retreat at the North Bridge in Salem*. Salem, Massachusetts: William Ives & George Pease, 1856.

Egle, William Henry, editor, *Some Pennsylvania Women during the War of the Revolution*, Harrisburg, Pennsylvania: Harrisburg Publishing Co., 1898.

Falkner, Leonard, *Captor of the Barefoot General*, August 1960 American Heritage Magazine, 11:5.

Fantina, Robert, *Desertion and the American Soldier, 1776-2006*. New York, New York: Algora Publishing, 2006.

Fischer, David, *Paul Revere's Ride*. New York, New York: Oxford Press, 1994.

Fischer, David Hackett, *Washington's Crossing*. New York, New York: Oxford Press, 2004.

Felch, William Farrand, George Atwell, H. Phelps Adams, and Francis Treelyan Miller, *The Connecticut Magazine, Vol. 9*. Hartford, Connecticut, 1905.

Fenn, Elizabeth A., *Pox Americana: The Great Smallpox Epidemic of 1775-82*. New York, New York: Hill & Wang, 2002.

Fisher, Dan, *Bringing Back the Black Robed Regiment*. Mustang, Oklahoma: Tate Publishing, 2013.

Fisher, David, *Bill O'Reilly's Legends and Lies: The Patriots*. New York, New York: Henry Holt & Company, 2016.

Flexner, James Thomas, *The Traitor and the Spy: Benedict Arnold and John Andre*. Syracuse, New York: Syracuse University Press, 1953.

Flexner, James Thomas, *Washington: The Indispensable Man*. New York, New York: New American Library, 1979.

Foster, Sophie Lee, *Revolutionary Reader, Reminiscences and Indian Legends*. Atlanta, Georgia: Byrd Printing Company, 1913.

Founders online National Archives.

Frank, Andrew, editor, *American Revolution: People and Perspectives*. Santa Barbara, California: ABC-CLIO, 2008.

Frank, Lisa Tendrich, editor, *An Encyclopedia of American Women at War: from the Home Front to the Battlefield*. Santa Barbara, California: ABC-CLIO, 2013.

Freeman, Lucy and Alma Bond, *America's First Woman Warrior: the Courage of Deborah Sampson*. Vadnais Heights, Minnesota: Paragon House, 1992.

Fremont-Barnes, Gregory editor, *Encyclopedia of the Age of Political Revolutions and New Ideologies, 1760-1815*. Westport, Connecticut: Greenwood Press, 2007.

Garden, Alexander, *Anecdotes of the Revolutionary War*. Charleston, South Carolina: A.E. Miller, 1822.

Green, Harry Clinton and Mary Wolcott Green. *The Pioneer Mothers of America*. New York, New York: G.P. Putnam & Sons, Knickerbocker Press, 1912.

Greene, Jerome A., *The Guns of Independence: The Siege of Yorktown, 1781*. New York, New York: Savas-Beatie, 2005.

Greene, Nelson, editor, *History of the Mohawk Valley: Gateway to the West 1614-1925*. Chicago, Illinois: S.J. Clarke, 1925.

Grizzard, Frank E. Jr., *George Washington A Biographical Companion*. Santa Barbara, California: ABC-CLIO, 2002.

Godfrey, Carlos Emmor, *The Commander in Chief's Guard, Revolutionary War*. Washington D.C.: Stevenson-Smith, 1904.

The Goyen Family Tree Newsletter 6 June, 1998. Website.

Haggard, Robert F., *The Nicola Affair: Lewis Nicola, George Washington, and American Military Discontent during the Revolutionary War*. Proceedings of the American Philosophical Society Vol. 146, No. 2, June 2002.

Hannafore, Phebe A., *Daughters of America on Women of the Century*. Boston, Massachusetts: B.B. Russell, 1883.

Hakim, Joy. *From Colonies to Country, 1735-1791*. New York, New York: Oxford University Press, 1993.

Harper's Monthly magazine December of 1864.

Harrell-Sesniak, Mary, *Hundred Plus Revolutionary War Obituaries and Death Notices*. Houston, Texas, 2010.

_____. *Harvard Alumni Veterans of the American Revolutionary War*. Boston, Massachusetts: Harvard Press, 1921.

Hartley, Cecil P., *Heroes and Patriots of the South.* Philadelphia, Pennsylvania: G.G. Evans, 1860.

Haven, Kendall F., *Voices of the American Revolution: Stories of Men, Women, and Children Who Forged Our Nation.* Westport, Connecticut: Greenwood Publishing, 2000.

Headley, Joel Tyler, *The Chaplains and Clergy of the Revolution.* New York, New York: Charles Scribner, 1864.

Hicks, George W., *Revolutionary War amid Southern Chaos.* Baltimore, Maryland: PublishAmerica, 2008.

Historical Register of the Colorado Society of the Sons of the American Revolution, November 1, 1905 to February 1, 1912.

_____, *History in the Making.* California State University, San Bernardino Journal of History, Vol. 9.

_____, Holden's Dollar Magazine, Vol. 1, Number 1, January 1, 1848.

Horick, Carl P., *A Gallant Defense: The Siege of Charleston,* Columbia, South Carolina: University of South Carolina Press, 2003.

Horry, Brig. Gen. P., *The Life of General Francis Marion a Celebrated Partisan officer in the Revolutionary War Against the British and Tories in South Carolina and Georgia.* Philadelphia, Pennsylvania: Joseph Allen, 1852.

Howland, Franklin, *A History of the Town of Acushnet, Bristol County, State of Massachusetts.* New Bedford, Massachusetts: Published by Author, 1907.

Hoyt, William Henry, *The Mecklenburg Declaration of Independence: A Study of Evidence showing that the Alleged Early Declaration of Independence is Spurious.* New York, New York: G. Putnam & Sons, 1907.

Hubbard, John, *Sketches of Border Adventures in the Life of Major Moses Van Campen.* New York, New York: Jno. S. Fillmore, 1842.

Hunsicker, Jennifer, *Young Andrew Jackson in the Carolinas: A Revolutionary Boy.* Charleston, South Carolina: History Press, 2014.

Hunter, Andrew, *Diary of Andrew Hunter.* Website.

Ireland, Corydon, *Harvard's Year of Exile,* Harvard Gazette, October 13, 2011.

Jennings, Francis, *America: Through Revolution to Empire.* New York, New York: Cambridge University Press, 2000.

Johnson, Kenneth D., *The Bloodied Mohawk: The American Revolution in the Words of Fort Planks Defenders and Other Mohawk Valley.* Rockland, Maine: Picton Press, 2000.

Johnston, Henry Phelps, Y*ale and Her Honor Roll in the American Revolution* New York, New York: Published by Author, 1888.

Johnson, Joseph, *Traditions and Reminiscences Chiefly of the American Revolution in the South.* Charleston, South Carolina: Walker & James, 1851.

Johnson, Kenneth D., *The Bloodied Mohawk: The American Revolution in the Words of Fort Planks Defenders and Other Mohawk Valley Partisans.* Camden, Maine: Picton Press, 2000.

Johnston, Henry Phelps, *The Storming of Stony Point on the Hudson.* New York, New York: James T. White, 1900.

Kapp, Frederick, *The Life of Frederick William Von Steuben.* New York, New York: Mason Brothers, 1859.

Kate Book. Com, a Website for Kates, by Kates, and About Kates.

Kelly, C. Brian, *Best Little Stories from the American Revolution.* Naperville, Illinois: Cumberland House, 1999.

Kennedy, Billy, *Women of the Frontier.* Greenville, South Carolina: Ambassador International, 2004.

Kilgannon, Corey, *Crossing the Delaware, More Accurately.* New York Times, December 23, 2011.

Landers, Howard Lee, *The Virginia Campaign and the Blockade and Siege of Yorktown.* Army War College Historical Section.

Landis, John B., *A Short History of Molly Pitcher, the Heroine of the Battle of Monmouth.* Carlisle, Pennsylvania: Cornman Printing Co. 1905.

Lanning, Michael, *African Americans in the Revolutionary War.* New York, New York: Kensington Press, 2000.

Lee, Charles, *Dictionary of National Biography.* New York, New York: MacMillan Co., 1909.

Leonard, Elizabeth, *All the Daring of the Soldier.* New York, New York: Penguin Books, 2001.

Leonard, Patrick J., *Ann Bailey: Mystery Woman Warrior of 1777.* MINERVA: Quarterly Report on Women and the Military, Vol. XI Nos. 3 & 4. 2.

Lightfoot, Marise Parrish, *Let the Drums Roll: Veterans and Patriots of the Revolutionary War Who Settled in Maury County, Tennessee.* Maury, Tennessee: Maury County Publisher, 1976.

Loprieno, Don, *The Enterprise in Contemplation: The Midnight Assault of Stony Point.* Berwyn Heights, Maryland: Heritage Books, 2004.

Lossing, Benson John, *Life of Washington Vol. 1.* New York, New York, Virtue and Company: 1860.

Lossing, Benson John, *The Pictorial Field-Book of the Revolution Vol I.* New York, New York: Harper & Brothers, 1852.

Lovett, Howard Meriwether, *Grandmother Stories from the Land of Used-to-Be.* Atlanta, Georgia: A.B. Caldwell, 1913.

Mahoney, Harry and Marjorie Locke Mahoney, *Gallantry in Action: A Biographic Dictionary of Espionage in the American Revolutionary War.* Lanham, Maryland: University Press of America, 1999.

Malcolm, Joyce Lee, *Peter's War: A New England Slave Boy and the American Revolution.* New Haven, Connecticut: Yale University Press, 2008.

Maupin, Judy, *Echoes from The Past.* Column of Historical and Genealogical Anecdotes, Stories and Family Notes. Calloway County, Kentucky.

Mayers, Robert A., *The Battle of the Short Hills.* Garden State Legacy.com, Issue 13, September 2011.

McCullough, David, *Seventeen Seventy-Six.* New York, New York: Simon & Schuster, 2005.

McDonald, Hugh, *Memoir by Hugh McDonald,* (extract) North Carolina University Magazine, December 1853, Vol. 11.

McGaugh, Scott, *Battlefield Angels: Saving Lives under Enemy Fire from Valley Forge to Afghanistan.* England: Osprey Publishing, 2011.

McIntosh, John H., *History of Elbert County, Georgia 1790-1935.* Nashville, Tennessee, Boyd Publishing, 1996.

Meriwether, Colyer, *Publications of the Southern History Association Vol. 1.* Washington D.C.: The Association, 1907.

Minardi, Margot, *Making Slavery History: Abolitionism and the Politics of Memory in Massachusetts.* New York, New York: Oxford Press, 2010.

Misenick, Paul R., *The Original American Spies: Seven Covert Agents of the Revolutionary War.* Jefferson, North Carolina: McFarland, 2014.

Moore, Frank, *Songs and Ballads of the American Revolution.* Bedford, Massachusetts: Applewood Books, 1856.

Moore, Horatio Newton, *The Life and Times of General Francis Marion.* Philadelphia, Pennsylvania: J.P. Lippincott, 1860.

Moran, Donald N., *Never Too Old: The Story of Captain Samuel Whittemore*. War History online, website.

Moran, Donald N., *Sergeant Elijah Churchill of the Second Continental Light Dragoons*. Article from April 2007 of the Liberty Tree Newsletter.

Moran, Donald, N, *The Storming of Stony Point*. Website.

Morgan, Robert, *On This Day: 365 Amazing and Inspiring Stories about Saints, Martyrs, and Heroes*. Nashville, Tennessee: Thomas Nelson, 1997.

Murray, Louise Welles, *A History of old Tioga Point and Early Athens, Pennsylvania*. Athens, Pennsylvania: Raeder Press, 1907.

Nelson, James L., *With Fire and Sword: The Battle of Bunker Hill and the Beginning of the American Revolution*. New York, New York: St. Martin's Press, 2011.

Nelson, Paul David, *Anthony Wayne, Soldier of the Early Republic*. Bloomington, Indiana: Indiana University Press, 1985.

Nevin, Alfred, editor, *Encyclopedia of the Presbyterian Church in the United States of America*. Philadelphia, Pennsylvania: Presbyterian Publishing, 1884.

_____, New England's Dark Day from the Weather Doctor Almanac, 2004.

Niles, Grace Greylock, *The Hoosac Valley*. New York, New York: Knickerbocker Press, 1912.

North Carolina Genealogy Webpage.

North, Sterling, *George Washington Frontier Colonel*. Minneapolis, MN: Quarto Publications, 2016.

New York Times Article 7 December, 1879.

Null, William C., *Colored Patriots of the American Revolution*. Boston, Massachusetts: Robert F. Wallcut, 1856.

O'Donald, Patrick, *The Untold Story of an Elite Regiment Who Changed the Course of the Revolution*. New York, New York: Atlantic Monthly Press, 2016.

_____, *The Official Roster of the Soldiers of the American Revolution Buried in the State of Ohio*. State of Ohio.

Quintal, George Jr., *Patriots of Color; African Americans and Native Americans at Battle Road & Bunker Hill*. Division of Cultural Resources Boston Natural Historical Park, 1996.

Patton, Jacob Harris, *A Popular History of the Presbyterian Church*. New York, New York: R.S. Mighill 7 Co., 1900.

_____, Peter Francisco, William and Mary College Quarterly Historical Magazine Vol. XIII, April, 1905, No. 4.

Pickering, Octavius, *The Life of Timothy Pickering, Vol. I*. Boston, MA: Little, Brown, and Company, 1867.

Porter, Joseph, editor, *Memoir of Gen. Henry Knox of Thomaston, Maine*. Bangor, Maine: Benjamin J. Burns, 1890.

Porter, Rev., President of the New England Historical Society, article: Antique News of Boston.

Potaski, Michael, Blackstone Valley Tribune article, Vol II, number 10, 5 December, 2008.

Powell, William S., editor, Dictionary *of North Carolina Biography: Vol. 5, P-S*. Chapel Hill, North Carolina: University of North Carolina Press.

Raphael, Ray, *Founders: The People Who Brought You a Nation*. New York, New York: The New Press, 2009.

Reiss, Dr. Oscar, *Medicine and the American Revolution*. Jefferson, North Carolina: McFarland, 1998.

_____, Report of the Committee Appointed to Revise the Soldier's Record, Salem, Massachusetts: Newcomb & Gauss, 1895.

Reynolds, Cuyler, *Hudson-Mohawk Genealogical and Family Memoirs, Vol. 1. And Vol. III.* New York, New York: Lewis Publishing Co., 1911.

Ricord, R.W., *History of Union County, New Jersey, Vol. 1-2.* New York, New York: New Jersey Historical Publishing, 1897.

Ripley's Believe it or Not! February 20, 1942.

Rockwell, Anne, *They Called Her Molly Pitcher.* New York, New York: Alfred A. Knopf, 2002.

Root, Mary Philotheta, Chapter Sketches, Connecticut D.A.R. *Patriots' Daughters, 1900. Chapter Sketches, Connecticut D.A.R. Patriots' Daughters.* New Haven, Connecticut: Connecticut Chapter of the D.A.R., 1900.

Roy-Sole, Monique, *Trois-Rivieres-A Tale of Tenacity.* Royal Canadian Geographic Society, May 23, 2009.

Ruddiman, John A., *Becoming Men of Some Consequence: Youth and Military Service in the Revolutionary War.* University of Virginia Press, 2014.

Russell, David Lee, *The American Revolution in the Southern Colonies.* Jefferson, North Carolina: McFarland, 2000.

Saunders, Robert L., *John Paul Jones: Finding the Forgotten Patriot.* Published by Author, 2009.

Savas, Theodore P. & J. David Dameron, *A Guide to the Battles of the American Revolution.* New York, New York: Savas-Beatie, 2006.

Schenck, David, *North Carolina 1780-81 being a History of the Invasion of the Carolinas by the British Army under Lord Cornwallis.* Raleigh, North Carolina: Edwards & Broughton, 1889.

Schroeder-Lossing, *Life and Times of Washington Vol II.* Albany, New York: M.M. Blecher, 1903.

Scott, John Thomas, *Nancy Hart: Too Good Not to Tell Again in Georgia Women: Their Lives and Times Vol. 1.* Athens, Georgia: University of Georgia Press, 2009.

Sears, Captain Clinton B., *A Genealogical Record of the Descendants of Captain Samuel Ransom of the Continental Army.* St. Louis, Mo.: Nixon-Jones, 1861.

Shattuck, Lemuel, *Memorials of the Descendants of William Shattuck.* Boston, Massachusetts: Dutton & Wentworth, 1855.

Shaw, Henry I. and Ralph W. Donnelly, *Blacks in the Marine Corps.* History and Museums Division, Headquarters, U.S. Marine Corps, 1976.

Simms, Jeptha R., *History of Schoharie County and Border Wars of New York, Vol. 2.* Albany, New York: Munsell & Taylor, 1845.

Simms, W. Gilmore, *The Life of Francis Marion.* New York, New York: Geo. F. Cooledge & Brother, 1811.

Smith, Doty, *History of Livingston County, New York 1678-1881.* Geneseo, New York: Geneseo, 1876.

Smith, Jean Edward, *John Marshall: Definer of a Nation.* New York, New York: Henry Holt & Company, 1996.

Smith, Robert, *The American Revolution and Righteous Community.* Columbia, South Carolina: The University of the South Carolina Press, 2007.

Smith, Samuel Abbot, *West Cambridge 1775.* Arlington, Massachusetts: Arlington Historical Society, 1974.

Solano, Connie, *Courageous Women: Thirty-Two Short Stories.* Tucson, Arizona: Wheatmark, 2011.

Sparks, Jared, *The Writings of George Washington.* Boston, Massachusetts: Russell, Odiorne, and Medcalf, 1837.

Stanley, Bill, *Fourth of July Celebrations Lost to History.* Norwich Bulletin, Jan. 29, 2008.

Stansfield, Charles A., *Haunted Vermont: Ghosts and Strange Phenomena of the Green Mountain State*. Machanicsburg, Pennsylvania: Stackpole Books, 2007.

Stone, William L., *The Campaign of Lieut. Gen. John Burgoyne*. Albany, New York: Joel Munsell, 1877.

Taylor, Alan, *The Divided Ground-Indians, Settlers, & Northern Borderland of the American Revolution*. New York, New York: Alfred A. Knopf, 2006.

Tenkotte, Paul, A., and James C. Claypool, editor, *The Encyclopedia of Northern Kentucky*. Lexington, Kentucky: The University Press of Kentucky, 2009.

Thacher, James, *A Military Journal during the American Revolutionary War, from 1775 to 1783*. Boston, Massachusetts: Cottons & Barnard, 1823.

Thompson, Parker C., *From Its European Antecedents to 1791—The United States Army Chaplaincy*. Washington D.C., Department of the Army, 1978.

Tiger, Caroline, *General Howe's Dog: George Washington, the Battle of Germantown, and the Dog who Crossed Enemy Lines*. New York, New York: Chamberlain Bros, 2005.

Tucker, Glenn, *Mad Anthony Wayne and the New Nation: The Story of Washington's Front-Line General*. Mechanicsburg, Pennsylvania: Stackpole Books, 1973.

_____, The United States Army Chaplaincy by United States Department of the Army. Office of the Chief of Chaplains. Published 1977.

The University Magazine, Vol. VIII, #1 New York January 1893.

Unvericht, Patti. *Ghosts & Hauntings of the Finger Lakes*. Charleston, South Carolina: Haunted America, 2012.

U.S. Civil War History & Genealogy-The Drummer Boys, genelogyforum.com.

Waddell, Jos. A., *Annals of Augusta County*. Staunton, Virginia: C. Russell Caldwell, 1902.

Weaver, Ethen Allen, editor, *Register of the Pennsylvania Society of the Sons of the Revolution, 1888-1898*. Published by the Society, 1908.

Watson, Henry C., *Daring Deeds of the Old Heroes of the Revolution*. Boston, Massachusetts: Lee & Shepard, 1893.

Wheeler, William Bruce and Lorri Glover, *Discovering the American Past: A Look at the Evidence, Vol I: to 1877*. Boston, Massachusetts: Cengage Learning, 2007.

Wildwood, Warren, *Thrilling Adventures Among the Early Settlers*. Philadelphia, Pennsylvania: J. Edwin Potter, 1866.

Williams, Charles F., *Genealogical Notes of the Williams and Gallup Families*. Boston, Massachusetts: Higgins Book Store, 1897.

Williams, Catherine, *Biography of Revolutionary Heroes*. Providence, Rhode Island: Published by Author, 1839.

Wilson, James Grant and John Fiske, *Appleton's Cyclopedia of American Biography, Vol 8*. New York, New York: D. Appleton and Company, 1918.

Woodbury, James T., *Speech delivered in the House of Representatives of Massachusetts, February 3, 1851 upon the question of granting two thousand dollars to aid the town of Acton in building a monument over the remains of Capt. Isaac Davis, Abner Hosmer, and Jas. Hayward, Acton Minute Men, killed at Concord fight, April 19, 1775*, (1851).

Worth, Richard, *Teetotalers and Saloon Smashers: The Temperance Movement and Prohibition*. Berkeley Heights, New Jersey: Enslow Publishers, 2009.

The WPA Guide to Kentucky the Bluegrass State by Federal Writer's Project.

Wright, Henry Parks, *Soldiers of Oakham, Massachusetts, in the Revolutionary War*. New Haven, Connecticut: The Tuttle, Morehouse, & Taylor Press, 1914.

_____, Young and Brave: Girls Changing History. Website.

Government Records:

American Revolution and War of 1812, Vol. 1. Ancestry.com database.

Book of American Revolutionary Soldiers, Archives 5th Ser. Vol 2. Archives State of New York.

Census records. Ancestry.com database.

Connecticut Town Birth Records. Ancestry.com database.

Connecticut Town Marriage Records pre-1870. Ancestry.com database.

Index of Obituaries, Massachusetts 1740-1800. Ancestry.com database.

Massachusetts Soldiers & Sailors in the War of Revolution Vols. 1. Boston 1902.

Massachusetts Soldiers & Sailors in the War of Revolution Vols. 12. Boston 1904.

Massachusetts, Wills & Probate Records 1635-1999, Vol. 74-75. Ancestry.com database.

New Hampshire, Death & Burial Records 1654-1949. Ancestry.com database.

New Jersey Marriage Records. Ancestry.com database.

North Carolina and Tennessee Revolutionary War Land Warrants. Ancestry.com database.

Pennsylvania Veterans Burial Cards 177-2012. Ancestry.com database.

Pennsylvania Province and State History, 1609-1790, Vol II. Ancestry.com database.

Pension List of 1792-1795. Ancestry.com database.

Revolutionary War Rolls in Penn. 1775-1778. Ancestry.com database.

Roster of Know Soldiers of the 6th Regiment North Caroline Line. Ancestry.com database.

Service of Connecticut Men in the War of the Revolution. Ancestry.com database.

State of North Carolina Archives, Revolutionary Army Accounts, 1995.

The United States Army Chaplaincy by United States Department of the Army. Office of the Chief of Chaplains. 1977.

U.S. Pension Records. Ancestry.com database.

U.S. Pension Roll of 1835. Ancestry.com database.

U.S. Pensioners 1818-1872. Ancestry.com database.

U.S. Revolutionary War Rolls 1775-1783. Ancestry.com database.

Kentucky Land Grants Vol. 1. Ancestry.com database.

INDEX

A
Adams, John, 24

Adans, Samuel, 8-9, 13

Aitkin, John (the painter), 120

Andre, Major John, 53, 75, 77

Arnold, Benedict, 26, 51, 63, 72, 75-77, 90, 94-95, 117

Ashbow, Samuel, 23-24

B
Bailey, Ann, 114

Baker, Sergeant, 69

Barney, Joshua, 126

Batherick, Mother, 21

Battle of: Bemis Heights; 51 Bennington; Black Mingo; 77 Blue Licks; Brandywine; 33-34, 50 Breed's Hill; 24 Brier Creek; 66 Brooklyn; 39 Bunker Hill; 11, 14, 23, 125, 127 Camden; 63, 74, 26 Cowpens; 33 Eutaw Springs; 95, 109, 126, 129 Fort Clinton; 50 Fort Griswold; 94-95, 127 Germantown; 33-34, 39, 50, 113 Great Bridge; 29 Guilford Courthouse; 30, 33, 89, 126 Hanging Rock; 74 Haw River; 88 Kings Mountain; 63, 79-83 Lexington & Concord; 13-16, 19-24, 28, 123, 126 Long Island; 42 Monmouth; 11, 32-33, 39, 44, 55, 58-59 Moore's Creek; 35, 37 Musgrove Mill; 74 Newark; 44 Newtown; 34 Oriskany; 128 Princeton; 31, 44, 127 Red Bank; 52 Rugeley's Mills; 82 Saratoga; 11, 31, 33, 72 Short Hills; 47, 128 Stony Point; 68-69, 111 Tory Hole; 93 Trenton; 41, 43 Trois-Rivers; 37 White Plains; 40, 45 Yorktown; 34, 85, 90-92, 94-96, 98-99, 109, 121, 123, 127, 130

Bettys, John, 117

Blain, James, 87-88

Bissell, Sergeant Daniel, 90

Bolling, Susanna, 98

Boone, Daniel, 60, 104

Boston Tea Party, 10-11

Bovie, Nicholas, 48

Bovie, Peter, 48

Brace, Jeffery (blind slave), 45

Bradlee, Nathaniel, 10

Brant, Captain Joseph, 122

Brown, Thomas, 90

Brown, William, 90

Burgoyne, General, 24, 51

C
Cabel, Joseph, 98

Cameron, Captain Charles, 57-58

Capers, James, 109

Champion, Deborah, 113

Charlestown, 58, 63, 71-72, 77, 126

Church, Dr. Benjamin, 27

Clark, Captain William, 129

Clark, George Rogers, 66

Clarke, Thomas, 50

Clinton, General George, 50

Clinton, General Henry, 50, 85, 91

Clinton, General James, 50

Coburn, Sampson, 125

Cock, John, 100

Congress, Continental, 13, 38, 110, 123, 128

Congress, Continental First, 6

Congress, Continental Second, 45

Constitution, 46

Cook, Lemuel, 114-115

Cornwallis, General Charles, 47-48, 63, 66, 78, 85, 97-99, 121, 130

Cummings, Pastor Charles, 122

Cummings, Samuel, 18-19

D

Dark Day, 72-73

Darragh, Lydia, 52-53

Davenport, John, 89

Deane, John, 97

Deanne, Silas, 120

Duncan, George, 66

Duncan, James, 96

E

Eaton, General Thomas, 66

Eaton, Reuben, 22

Elliott, Anna, 114

Ellis, Pastor John, 127

Emerson, Pastor William, 125

Expedition, Penobscot, 125

F

Farnsworth, David, 61

Farrow, Rosanna, 83

Ferguson, Captain Patrick, 52, 79

Field, Lewis, 66-67

Fleury, Lt. Colonel, 69

Flora, William, 29

Flower, Zephon, 110

Fort: Niagara; 48, 105 Mifflin; 49 Montgomery; 50 Stanwix; 11, 48 Washington; 128

Franklin, Benjamin, 32, 46, 106-107

Franklin, Robert; 48

Fransciso, Peter, 32-34

Fraser, General Simon, 59

Frazee, Aunt Betty, 47-48

French and Indian War, 5, 13

Futrell, Nathan, 128

Fulton, Sarah, 10-11

G

Gage, General, 13-14

Geiger, Emily, 92-93

Girty, Simon, 67

Goodard, John, 110

Goddard, Mary Katharine, 45

Gowens, George, 114

Gore, Sammy, 7-8

Greene, Nathanael, 9, 57, 72, 85, 92-93

Guyer, John, 37

Guyer, Peter, 37

H

Hale, Rev. Enoch, 125

Hale, Nathan, 125

Hall, Primus, 100-101

Hamilton, Alexander, 57, 95-96

Hancock, John, 13, 24

Hart, Nancy, 64-65

Harvard, 22, 29

Hayward, James, 20

Heard, Stephen, 63-64

Heart, Purple, 92

Henry, Patrick, 32

Hessians, 31-32, 43, 72

Hill, Henry, 11-12

Hill, Nicholas, 11-12

Hopkinson, Francis, 57

Horry, Colonel Peter, 97

Howe, General William, 31, 47, 53

I

Independence, Declaration of, 32, 38, 45

Independence, Resolution of, 38

Indians: Cherokee; 100 Iroquois; 38 Seneca; 101-102

Invalid Regiment, 110

J

Jackson, Andrew, 103-104

Johnson, Joseph, 122

Johnston, Nicholas, 58

Jones, Horatio, 101-102

Jones, John Paul, 46-47

Jones, Rolling, 109

K

Kate, Mammy, 63-64

King George III, 5-6, 11, 14, 16, 19, 32, 37, 58, 120

Knight, Richard, 37

Knox, Henry, 28-29

L

Lafayette, General, 55, 93, 98, 127

Lane, Anna Maria, 113

Langston, Dicey, 115-116

Lash, 116-117, 120

Latham, Captain William, 94-95

Lee, Paul Ram, 109

Lee, Colonel William, 76, 88

Lee, General Charles, 42

Liberty Tree, 8

Lilly, Theophilus, 7

Lincoln, General, 127

M

Mackey, Charles, 85-87

Mackey, Lydia, 85-87

Marion, Colonel Francis, 70-71, 77

Marshall, John, 56-57

Martin, John, 50

Martin John Nicholas, 71

Massacre: Boston; 6 Cherry Valley; 105 Wyoming Valley; 34-35, 60

Mayes, Benjamin, 113

McArthur, Philip, 112

McDonald, Hugh, 35-36

McWhorter, Alexander, 61

Mengis, Colonel Return Jonathan 44

Mersereau, Joshua, 38

Merit, Badge of Military, 92

Miles, Private John, 129

Miller, James, 15

Minutemen, 17-18

Molly, Captain, 41

Morgan, Daniel, 51

Morgan, James, 127

Morrell, Captain John, 54

Morton, John, 38

Murphy, John, 74

Murphy, Timothy, 41

Murray, Mary, 39

N

Nelson, Moses, 60

Nevelling, Rev. John Wesley Gilbert, 125

Nickerson, Jonathan, 40-41

Nicola, Lewis, 110

O

Olney, Captain Stephen, 128

P

Paine, Thomas, 32

Paulding, John, 75-76

Peale, Charles W., 10

Pensell, Henry, 60

Pensell, John, 60

Percy, General, 22

Percy Pierre Francois, 116

Pickering, Colonel Thomas, 100-101, 123

Pierce, Samuel, 16

Pitcher, Molly, 58-59

Prewett, Joshu, 119

Pompey, 68-69

Pyle, Doctor John, 87-88

Q

Quaker, 9, 33, 111, 129

Quaker gun, 82

R

Rall, Colonel, 43

Ransom, George, 34-35, 49

Reynolds, Henry, 111-112

Reynolds, Phoebe, 111-112

Richardson, Ebenezer, 7-8

Roberts, Richard, 130

Rover, Jemmy the, 99

Royal, Isaac, 46-47

Rush, Doctor Benjamin, 116

S

Sanford, Chaplain David, 115

St. Clair, Sally, 69-70, 114

Sampson, Deborah, 114

Savannah, Siege of, 63, 70

Scalping, 48, 73-74

Seider, Christopher, 7-9

Shreve, Colonel Israel, 111

Simpson, Ann, 113

Smallpox, 91, 104, 120, 122

Smith, Colonel Daniel, 93-94

Smith, Rev. Robert, 58

Smith, Lt. Colonel Francis, 21

Snell, Peter, 126

Snowball fight, 29-30, 57

Spring, Pastor Samuel, 26

Spy, 26-27, 39, 75-77, 117

Sullivan Expedition, 39

Sullivan, General John, 11, 35

Sumter, General Thomas, 74, 93

T

Tarleton, Lt. Colonel Banastre, 33, 70-71, 78-79, 86-87, 97

Tarrant, Sarah, 15

Tavern, Cooper's, 20

Tavern, White's, 42

Taylor, George, 126

Thacher, Doctor James, 109-110, 130

Townsend, Sarah, 72

Trask, Israel, 29-30

Turtle, 44-45

Tyler, Bishop, 88-89

V

Valley, Forge, 11, 31, 36-37, 55-57, 120

Van Doren, John, 111

Van Doren, Martha, 111

Van Wart, John, 75-76

Visscher, Frederick, 77

Von Steuben, Baron, 12, 55, 57

W

Wagner, Joseph, 134

Wallace, Sally, 54

Wallace, Samuel, 50-51

Washington, George; 9-11, 14, 24-31, 35, 37, 39-40, 42-43, 46, 49, 52-53, 55, 57, 59, 61, 63, 69, 75, 74, 76-77, 82, 85 90, 93, 98-101, 105-107, 109-111, 113, 115, 117, 120-121, 125, 129, crossing the Delaware; 31, 39, 43, 118-119 false teeth; 91

Washington's Life Guard, 105

Wayne, General Anthony, 99

Webster, Samuel, 50-51

West, Pastor Samuel, 26-27

West Point, 41, 44, 49, 68, 75-77, 110, 117

Wheatley, Phillis, 9

Wheeler, Isaac, 121

Whitall, Mrs., 52

White, Ammi, 16

Whittemore, Cuff, 24

Whittemore, Samuel, 19-20

Whiting, Captain Leonard, 18

Williams, David, 75-76

Wilson, Zaccheus, 77-78

Wright, David, 17-19

Wright Prudence Cummings, 17-19

Y

Yankee Doodle, 22

Z

Zane, Elizabeth, 104-105

www.ingramcontent.com/pod-product-compliance
Lightning Source LLC
Chambersburg PA
CBHW081355230426
43667CB00017B/2836